577 *

Wildlife Watch

Moorlands & Uplands in Summer

Published by
The Reader's Digest Association Limited
London · New York · Sydney · Montreal

Contents

Wildlife habitats and havens

Upland watch

Animals and plants in focus

Moorland watch

Introduction

Summer in both moorland and upland is a season of rich colour. Saturated by summer rain, the grass retains the vivid green of spring while the dark heather begins to glow with purple and pink flowers. Clumps of gorse flare yellow on the hillsides amid the green fronds of bracken and stark outcrops of crystalline rock glitter in the sun. Spectacular masses of ragged grey and white cloud tower into skies of clear, rain-washed blue, casting dark, mobile shadows that leap and race over the hills and valleys. To stand on a high crag and survey such a scene is a truly memorable experience, made the more precious by its fleeting magic, for sooner or later the clouds will break and the rain will fall.

The soft sand of many heathlands is easily excavated by mining bees. Their crater-like burrows can pepper any bare patches of ground between the heather.

Restricted to upland regions such as the Scottish Highlands and Lake District, the mountain sorrel flowers in July and August in damp, rocky places.

The mewing call of the buzzard often draws attention to its broad-winged silhouette as it soars high over summer moorland looking for prey.

Acid soils

Rain is one of the defining characteristics of the higher altitudes in the British Isles. Prevailing south-westerly winds ensure a steady supply of moist air moving in from the Atlantic, and as this moist air is pushed upward over high ground it becomes cooler, making its moisture condense into clouds and rain. In some upland regions, such as western Scotland, the Lake District and Dartmoor, the rain can seem relentless, even in high summer. Yet the rain is largely responsible for the character of the terrain and, in particular, the broad expanses of bleak but glorious wild landscape we call moorland (see pages 12–17).

Moorland is dominated by low-growing plants such as heathers, bilberry, bracken and purple moor-grass (see pages 79–84), which are able to thrive in acidic, infertile soils. Such soils are partly created by the high rainfall, which washes any soluble, alkaline plant nutrients out of the earth and into the streams that flow down to the valleys. This process can even create pockets of acid soil on top of highly alkaline limestone in regions such as the Yorkshire Dales. Where the bedrock is granite (see pages 24–27) or sandstone there may be few alkaline minerals available to be dissolved.

The resulting acid soils in uplands make hostile environments for organisms that help organic matter to decompose, such as earthworms and soil bacteria, so plant remains do not decay properly or release nutrients into the soil. Instead, they build up as peat, which can reach immense thicknesses in the acidic swamps known as bogs or mires (see pages 18–23). In some places, these bogs cover vast areas with waterlogged bog moss and cotton-grass, punctuated with dark, peaty pools – a habitat so lacking in plant nutrients that some plants have evolved ways of catching and digesting insects (see pages 123–125).

Even on relatively dry terrain, the acidity and infertility of the land makes it unsuitable for the softer, more demanding plants that flourish on the richer valley soils. So in any moorland landscape there is a sharp distinction between the relatively lush vegetation of the valley floors and the heather and bracken of the hillsides. The boundary is often

Foxes often hunt on high, open moorland in summer, looking for voles, rabbits, ground birds and carrion. Moorland-dwelling foxes usually retreat to lower ground for the winter.

Peat bogs in summer often swarm with bloodsucking mosquitoes that have hatched from the bog pools, and they attract a number of insect-eating birds.

The delicate silver-studded blue butterfly is nearly always associated with lowland heaths, where it feeds on heather and gorse.

marked by dry-stone walls that divide the fertile valley farmland from the rough grazing of the wild, open hills.

Seasonal visitors

As the summer sun warms the moorland, it starts to buzz with insect life. Many of these insects are biting flies, such as midges and mosquitoes, but the flowering heather also attracts bees as well as butterflies (see pages 76–78 and 118–120). In their turn, the insects attract insect-eating birds, which take advantage of the seasonal wealth of food to breed.

Much of this breeding activity takes place in the spring, but in the far north some birds, such as the snow bunting, delay egg-laying until early summer so that their nestlings benefit from the boom in the insect population. Many moorland-breeding waders, such as the golden plover and dotterel, also have breeding seasons that extend into summer, and can be seen in the dramatic breeding plumage that they lose at the end of the season.

Summer bird visitors provide food for some charismatic birds of prey, including the powerful peregrine falcon (see pages 102–107) and the merlin, Britain's smallest bird of prey, which snatches meadow pipits, wheatears and other small birds in mid-air as it flies fast and low over the heather. The merlin shares its breeding territory with the much larger hen harrier, another moorland specialist. Unlike the merlin, it hunts not only small birds but also mammals, such as voles and young rabbits, with a slow, floating flight.

Summer grazing

The red deer of the Scottish Highlands (see pages 86–91) range high into the mountains to graze the moorland grasses and nibble the young heather shoots. Elsewhere, the largest grazing animals are likely to be native ponies (see pages 44–49). Those that live in the wild are allowed to graze wherever they wish but probably would not survive today without human intervention and management. Although these ponies are basically domestic animals run wild, many – such as those that roam the moorland of Exmoor – are well adapted to cope with rough grazing and the harsh upland climate, and have probably been living in the uplands since the last Ice Age.

At that time their main enemies would have been wolves – moorland and upland areas were the last refuges of these powerful predators in Britain. Today

Heathers are the characteristic plants of both moorland and heath, flowering in late summer. The Dorset heath is a rare species found only in south-west England.

The summer breeding plumage of the moorland-nesting dunlin is much more striking than the grey and white plumage it displays on coasts and estuaries in winter.

The yellow stripe on its back identifies this toad as a natterjack, a rare and threatened species that favours sandy heathlands and coastal dunes.

the largest ground predator in the uplands is the fox, which ranges high into the hills in summer and can often be seen picking its way through the heather on open moorland. In the Scottish Highlands its chief rivals for prey are the wildcat – a rare, shy, elusive creature that hunts almost exclusively at night – and the elegant pine marten (see pages 50–55), which is gradually increasing in numbers after decades of persecution. In Wales, the pine marten's relative the polecat survives in upland regions. It was once known as the foul-mart because of its strong smell.

Heathland magic

The heather that is such a conspicuous feature of high moorland is also the dominant plant of heathland and indeed the origin of the landscape's name. Heaths can look very like moors, but they occur in the lowlands where the climate is much warmer and drier. They owe their existence to sandy or gravelly soils, which are so free-draining that plant nutrients are washed down beyond the reach of small plants. Trees can still grow, but their removal by the lowland farmers of long ago created the open heaths we know today (see pages 30–35).

Technically, heathland is an impoverished, unproductive habitat, but a visit to a heath in summer is always a rewarding experience. The broad stretches of flowering gorse and heather are often punctuated by patches of birch or pine woodland and small bogs, complete with carnivorous plants and moisture-loving orchids (see pages 121–122). The diversity of plant life offers habitats for a variety of insect life, including grasshoppers, crickets, beetles, several specialised butterflies and many species of dragonflies. The warm sandy soil is also ideal for reptiles, which are scarce in the cool uplands. In summer, lizards are numerous on some heaths and frequently seen. They provide prey for the rare smooth snake and the far more common, but always exciting, adder (see pages 70–75).

Heathland also has its bird specialities, such as the skulking Dartford warbler and the far more conspicuous, elegant and noisy stonechat. Displaying tree pipits and woodlarks fill the warm air with song, which is sometimes cut short by the deadly strike of the bird-hunting hobby, a summer visitor that is one of the swiftest and most elegant of falcons (see pages 64–69). Yet the most memorable experience of heathland in summer may occur after sunset, when the strange mechanical churring of the nightjar sounds through the thickening, heather-scented dusk and the bird itself flashes through the twilight like some giant moth as it hawks for insects well into the gathering night.

◄ One of the commonest birds of the uplands, the meadow pipit is regularly preyed upon by airborne hunters, such as the merlin and hen harrier.

▲ A tough, low-growing plant of the Arctic, mountain avens forms mats of white flowers at high altitudes in northern Scotland and Ireland.

Welsh upland is the last stronghold of the polecat in Britain. The wild ancestor of the domestic ferret, a polecat can catch and kill animals as large as hares.

Wildlife habitats and havens

- Moorland – untamed wilderness
- Peat bogs
- Granite uplands
- In and around a dry-stone wall
- Heaths – sandy suntraps
- The Peak District – land of hill and dale

Moorland – untamed wilderness

Usually situated far from human habitation, moors provide refuge for many animals and plants that possess the hardy qualities needed to thrive in rough terrain. Sharp-eyed birds of prey scan the heather as red deer roam and graze.

Most moorland comprises tracts of treeless, uncultivated terrain, which can seem bleak and hostile, especially in the wind and rain. Yet its austere nature and broad horizons evoke a sense of wilderness unrivalled in Britain, and several national parks have been established to preserve its remote, untamed quality. The vegetation is dominated by low-growing shrubs that are adapted to the relatively high annual rainfall and the acidic, nutrient-poor soils. A whole range of plants may thrive, each with its own community of associated animal life.

In the past, some moorland was cultivated, but the harsh climate, rough terrain and impoverished soils make such farming uneconomic today. The moors are still important to farmers, though, for grazing flocks of tough upland sheep.

Cleared land

Although moorland may look entirely natural, appearances are deceptive. Following the retreat of the glaciers at the end of the last Ice Age, much of upland Britain was colonised by trees such as pine and oak. During the Neolithic period, however, people started felling the trees for fuel and timber, and to clear the land for grazing animals and growing crops.

Little bigger than a blackbird, but with longer wings, a male merlin uses a perch to scan for prey. This fast-flying falcon includes the North York Moors among its strongholds.

A mountain hare bolts for safety at high speed. In the summer, it can be distinguished from a brown hare by its all-white tail.

▲ Chickweed wintergreen is a common perennial on some Scottish moorlands, but scarce in northern England. It flowers from May to August.

▼ Cowberry, a low-growing relative of bilberry, favours upland moors. Its clusters of pale pink or white flowers appear during May and June.

▲ Golden plovers can be found on upland moors from March to August. They nest among short vegetation and on recently burnt patches of ground.

The exploitation of the land stopped the trees regenerating and now flocks of upland sheep have the same effect. So although some moorland is almost certainly natural in origin, the treeless landscape of today owes a lot to the influence of man. Despite this, moorland is a haven for wild plants and animals, and thoroughly worthy of the protection it receives.

The character of moorland differs according to the region in which it is located. It also varies at a more local level, and the vegetation and associated wildlife of a particular moor can change dramatically within the space of a few hours' walk.

Climate and geology are two of the most important factors influencing moorland vegetation, with the annual rainfall, elevation – which affects temperature – and drainage of the site being particularly significant. On moors where the annual rainfall is moderate – from 600 to 1100 millimetres (24–43ins) per year – members of the heather family often dominate. These heather moors are, in many ways, the upland counterpart of lowland heath.

Ling and heather

On relatively dry, free-draining soils, by far the most common plant is ling, which is often referred to simply as 'heather'. It dominates the landscape of many moorlands, such as the North York Moors where, when it is in full bloom in August, whole hillsides are covered in a pinkish-purple carpet of flowers.

Bright, purple-flowered bell heather often occurs with ling on dry terrain, but where the ground is damp both species are replaced by the pink-flowered cross leaved heath.

▼ There are few natural sights to rival flowering heather moors in July and August. Splashes of yellow gorse provide a vibrant contrast.

► Adders are fairly common on all but the wettest of moors. Sensitive to sound and vibrations, they normally keep out of the way of walkers. Even so, it is best to wear sturdy boots that cover the ankles.

DANGER!

Upland moorland can be unforgiving terrain and you should never forget that the weather can change quickly. When walking, always take a compass and map and inform someone of your proposed route.

Wildlife habitats and havens

MANAGING MOORS FOR RED GROUSE

If one bird species has become synonymous with moorland habitat it is the red grouse. Indeed, vast areas of Britain's uplands are managed specifically to encourage this valuable gamebird. Management includes the practice of systematically burning patches of heather moorland. Although this may seem like a devastation of land, it encourages a fresh growth of young heather shoots, which are an important source of food for the grouse. Burning is undertaken on a rotational basis, which creates a mosaic of land where the vegetation is at different heights, providing vital cover for the birds as well as food.

The routine burning of moorland clearly benefits some forms of wildlife at the expense of others and species that show poor dispersal, or need long-term habitat stability, are unlikely to survive.

However, surveys of upland birds undertaken in the 1980s have revealed some unexpected beneficiaries of grouse moor management. Surprisingly, recently burned areas of heather, where the ground is still blackened by fire, often harbour far greater densities of nesting waders than can be found in neighbouring patches where the vegetation is lush.

In addition to the burning regimes, land management for red grouse has had repercussions for other species. In the past, those that were perceived as threats to the grouse or its eggs were often killed. Although such persecution is now against the law, the hen harrier has been effectively removed from some moors in England and Scotland.

◄ Upland moors are the haunt of red grouse, a mainstay of the game industry. The grouse depends on heather for food and cover, and some moors are managed solely with the grouse's needs in mind.

▲ A grouse moor shows a combination of mature vegetation, new growth and sparse clearings, all of which are needed for the birds to thrive. Young heather shoots appear within a year or so of burning.

◄ Areas of heather moors are burned in rotation to destroy old, woody growth and promote fresh new shoots. Fires seldom run out of control as the spread of the blaze is carefully monitored. The margins of the fire are beaten to slow down the flames.

◄ In Scotland and parts of northern England, wildcats have begun to spread to moorland, where they hunt mountain hares, small rodents and birds. These notoriously shy creatures keep to dense cover and are rarely seen.

► The emperor moth is found on heather moors. The larger female, seen here, may attract males by emitting a pheromone – a powerful scent that drifts on the breeze, drawing male moths from far away.

Flowers and berries

Open patches of ground are frequently colonised by colourful lichens, and the ground is often dotted with yellow, four-petalled tormentil flowers and the tiny white stars of heath bedstraw.

Typical of many areas of heather moor is the presence of low-growing, berry-bearing plants such as cowberry, crowberry and bilberry. At moderate altitudes, in places where the soil is particularly acidic and free-draining, bilberry can dominate the vegetation to the extent of forming a bilberry moor. Bilberry does not thrive on grouse moors that are regularly burned, so the plant is probably not as widespread as it might otherwise be. As a result, moorland plants that like the cover bilberry creates, such as chickweed wintergreen and dwarf cornel, also have a distinctly patchy distribution.

Several species of grasses and related plants occur on moorland. These include heath sedge, heath rush, wavy hair-grass, purple moor-grass and mat-grass. They can dominate the scenery in places that do not suit ling and heathers.

The presence of grazing sheep can have a dramatic effect upon vegetation. Unlike heathers, grasses are well adapted to recover from grazing but extreme grazing pressure can discourage even them, leaving inedible rushes as the dominant plants.

Upland moors receive much more rainfall than lowlands at similar latitudes, even in summer. Since many moorlands lie over hard, impervious rocks, the water flows downhill and accumulates at the bottoms of valleys instead of draining into the ground.

Where such valleys remain permanently waterlogged, bogs dominated by *Sphagnum* moss usually develop. Often known as bog-moss, *Sphagnum* can absorb large volumes of

▶ A female hen harrier brings food to her young in their nest on the ground. The male looks very different, with striking grey and white plumage.

▼ Moorland is often dotted with rocky outcrops and shrubs stunted by the constant wind, such as this hawthorn bush.

◄ Fir clubmoss is a surprisingly hardy, non-flowering plant. A perennial evergreen, it can be found on moors throughout the year.

▼ Male black grouse gather on communal display grounds in spring and summer to strut around and fight mock battles as the females watch from nearby.

water, extracting all the nutrients it needs and acidifying the water in the process. This makes the bog a hostile place for most plants, but nevertheless, highly adapted species, such as butterworts, bog asphodel and sundews, can be found among patches of bog myrtle, cotton grass, black bog-rush and white beak-sedge. Owing to the watery conditions, dead plant matter does not decompose but builds up as peat, raising the level of the bog year upon year.

Insect life

Moorland cannot support the diversity of invertebrate life found in lowland regions, but limited diversity does not necessarily mean scarcity. Some species are plentiful. Even on dull days, many beetles, spiders and slugs may be seen, and when the sun is out the flowers attract nectar-feeding butterflies. Dark green fritillaries are regular visitors to moorland, and the large heath, Scotch argus and small mountain ringlet are true upland butterflies, found only in northern Britain.

Male emperor and northern eggar moths can also be seen flying over the moors on sunny days, and both species are occasionally mistaken for butterflies. The flying adults can be quite conspicuous, but it takes a keen eye to spot the moth caterpillars hidden among the vegetation.

Flies of various species – including mosquitoes and biting midges – are abundant. Many breed in the upland streams and bog pools, overwintering as eggs or larvae and emerging to plague other animals in summer.

Breeding birds

Apart from supporting healthy populations of common frogs, the seasonal abundance of insects attracts large numbers of birds, which rely on the insect life to provide food for their young. Moors are vital nesting grounds for the majority of waders that breed in Britain, including lapwing, curlew, dunlin, redshank and golden plover. The evocative calls of the curlew and golden plover are among the most memorable features of moorland in summer.

The wealth of insect life also explains the presence of meadow pipits. Their 'tseet-tseet' calls as they flutter erratically into the air are a familiar sound of summer moorland.

Meadow pipits are a staple food of several predatory birds, particularly Britain's smallest bird of prey, the dashing merlin – a small,

Scottish red deer roam the open moors in summer, when the grasses, heather and lichens on which they feed are abundant.

Bogbean flourishes in boggy flushes on moorland, and often grows best where its roots lie in standing water. This plant flowers in May and June.

agile falcon that specialises in hunting over open moorland. Other airborne hunters include the hen harrier, which keeps low over the ground, and the day-flying short-eared owl.

Moorland mammals

The main prey of the hen harrier and short-eared owl is the field vole, which often occurs on moorland in large numbers. It is the staple food for so many upland predators that fluctuations in its fortunes can make all the difference between success and failure for breeding hawks and owls. A boom in the vole population spells success, but if voles are scarce, the birds may not be able to raise any young at all.

Voles are hard to spot as they feed beneath the moorland vegetation, but larger mammals can be watched from some distance as they move over the open terrain. Foxes, for example, are often to be seen trotting along in broad daylight, their progress causing scurrying

alarm among any mountain hares they encounter. The most spectacular of the moorland animals, however, are red deer. Despite being originally woodland dwellers, these magnificent mammals have adapted to live on open terrain, and many now flourish on the highest, most remote and impoverished of Scottish moorlands.

The lower slopes of the Cairngorms are cloaked with moorland. Peat bogs may form in areas of poor drainage.

WILDLIFE WATCH

Where can I see moorland?

1 The Shetland Islands
These are mainly moorland, but the best sites are on Unst. At Hermaness in the north, a National Nature Reserve (NNR) protects the moors that support breeding red-throated divers as well as waders.

2 Mainland Orkney
Many areas of Orkney are moorland regions, but one of the best is the RSPB reserve of Birsay Moor. Hen harriers, short-eared owls and merlins can be seen, plus a variety of moorland flowers.

3 The Flow Country, Northern Scotland
This vast area is fairly inaccessible, which has probably helped to preserve it. Limited access is available at Forsinard RSPB reserve, where breeding birds include divers as well as the hen harrier and greenshank.

4 The Lake District National Park, Cumbria
The Lake District has large tracts of moorland, but the pressure of visitors means that nesting birds are wary and hard to find. However, a visit to one of the remoter regions in summer may be rewarded by the sight of a merlin, a ring ouzel or even a golden eagle.

5 North York Moors National Park, North Yorkshire
This region includes some of the most conspicuously managed grouse moors in Britain and is home to high densities of red grouse. Breeding waders include lapwing, snipe, redshank and golden plover, which can be found from May to July. The heather is at its best from mid-July to late August.

6 Dartmoor and Exmoor National Parks, Devon
These national parks are the southernmost outposts of moorland habitat in Britain. Although popular with visitors, they still harbour a good range of breeding birds, including dunlin and a few red grouse on Dartmoor. The bog plant communities are generally rich and diverse.

Peat bogs

Mosses naturally flourish in these waterlogged conditions, and other types of wildlife have adapted in unusual ways – from the insect-eating butterwort to a spider that walks on water.

Waterlogged and relatively acidic, peat bogs are hostile environments for many forms of life. Some of the plants that live on them have developed amazing ways of gathering the nutrients they need for survival and several animals have evolved equally strange adaptations and habits. As a result, rare and unusual plants and creatures may be discovered on any peat bog, including flesh-eating plants, scuba-diving spiders and birds that 'sing' with their tails.

Bog formation

Peat bogs develop where poor drainage or high rainfall allow rainwater to accumulate at the surface. Rainwater is a weak acid, which normally dissolves plant nutrients in the soil, becoming neutral or alkaline in the process. If it falls on a region of hard, impervious rock, however, there may be few nutrients available, so the water stays acid and low in minerals. Even if the underlying rock is alkaline

Vast, undisturbed peat bogs in the Scottish Highlands are the main British refuge for nesting greenshank – elegant, long-legged waders.

limestone, as in parts of western Ireland, high rainfall may overwhelm the alkaline groundwater, which then has no influence on the surface vegetation. So all the plants must be able to cope with waterlogged, nutrient-poor, weakly acid conditions.

The plant life of a peat bog is dominated by spongy *Sphagnum* mosses. These plants can absorb immense amounts of water and extract the few minerals in it by replacing them with hydrogen. This makes the water even more acid and poorer in nutrients, which in turn makes survival harder for other plants.

The oxygen-demanding bacteria that normally rot down organic material cannot survive in the waterlogged, acidic conditions, so plants that grow in the bog do not decompose when they die. Instead, dead plant material accumulates and new plants simply grow on top of the remains of the old ones. Over hundreds, even thousands, of

years, the weight of new plants on top of the preserved plant remains gradually compresses them into peat.

There are several different kinds of bog. In parts of the Scottish Highlands and in much of the far west of Ireland, extensive layers of *Sphagnum* moss can form vast blanket bogs that stretch to the horizon in all directions. By contrast, small, soggy depressions on wet heathland, such as are found in the New Forest and on Surrey heaths, often contain valley bogs.

▼ Plants, such as these lichens and mosses, can grow in the impoverished conditions of peat bogs thanks to evolutionary adaptations that enable them to gather nutrients.

► Set against a backdrop of the Pass of Glencoe, and flanked by Beinn a' Chrulaiste and Stob Dearg, Rannoch Moor is a vast expanse of peat bog. Where erosion has occurred, the stumps of ancient pines are exposed, revealing that the region was wooded in the past.

▲ *Sphagnum* moss is capable of absorbing many times its own weight of water. When the moss dies, the waterlogged remains build up and eventually form bog peat.

DANGER!

The twin hazards of sucking mud and open water make bogs very dangerous places. Make sure you stick to designated paths and boardwalks, and do not venture out on to boggy ground alone.

The rare Rannoch-rush, which is related to the lily family, is confined to acid pools on Rannoch Moor in Perthshire. The plant has vanished from other localities because of drainage, peat cutting and the pressures of afforestation.

Tufted seed heads of common cotton grass are a frequent sight on peat bogs in summer. This species grows only on waterlogged ground that is too soft to be safely walked on.

Where conditions encourage the rapid growth of bog mosses, the amassing peat may spread out over the surface of a stream or other small expanse of water on the valley floor, and the result is a quaking bog, or quagmire.

Very high rainfall can transform valley bogs into great domes of peat and living moss known as raised bogs. Tregaron Bog in mid-Wales, for example, was once a lake fed by the River Teifi. Climatic changes, and in particular increased rainfall, enabled *Sphagnum* moss to spread over the lake and form deep layers of moss peat. Over the centuries new plants have grown on the peat, raising the bog surface above the original groundwater level. As a result, the top of the bog obtains all its water from rainfall, and is a very nutrient-poor habitat.

Open landscapes

Tree seedlings cannot become established in waterlogged, acid peat, and as bogs grow upward they tend to overwhelm and kill any existing trees. So bog landscapes are typically open, undulating carpets of bog mosses and other low plants.

Several species of *Sphagnum* moss may occur together, creating a diverse palette of colours with a background wash of ochre, amber and green, splashed with richer, more vivid tones of claret, crimson and magenta.

Polytrichum is another common moss in peat bogs. It is easily recognised by its stems, which are more erect than those of *Sphagnum* and bear radiating, pointed green leaves. The loosely clustered stems clump together to form soft, domed pillows, with apparently spiky leaf whorls.

Mosses lack colourful flowers, but they produce spore-filled capsules that are borne above the foliage on slender stalks. Peculiar blobs of orange-yellow 'jelly' on pale stalks are the caps of an

The great sundew is one of three sundew species that may be found growing on bogs. Its meagre diet is supplemented by nutrients from insects that are trapped and digested by its sticky leaves.

Comparatively few vertebrates live on peat bogs throughout the year. However, palmate newts are able to tolerate both the relatively acidic conditions and a supply of invertebrate food that is seasonal at best.

NATURAL RESOURCE

The traditional value of peat bogs to local communities was limited because the marshy conditions restricted access along with most forms of forestry, agriculture and development. Dried peat – or turf – can be burnt as fuel and in the past this is what made it a valuable resource for people who did not have the option of using firewood or coal.

Modern machinery has enabled peat to be harvested on an industrial scale for use in power plants and huge quantities are also now used in horticulture – adding peat improves the texture of soil and compost. Yet peat develops so slowly that large-scale harvesting is unsustainable, as well as destructive of the habitat, and campaigners have been fighting long and hard for peat bogs to be conserved rather than exploited.

Peat cutters often expose the blackened remains of trees that have been buried by the peat. These 'bog oaks' once grew in forests that were smothered by the peat and may be thousands of years old. Preserved by the swampy, acidic conditions of the bog, the timber is extremely hard when dry, and is much prized by wood turners and other craftsmen.

Even after centuries below the surface, bog oaks can be almost perfectly preserved. Only when they are exposed to the air does the process of decay begin.

unusual fungus, the bog beacon (also known as swamp candles and orange beacon).

Dense tufts of sedges and rushes sprout from among the mosses and midsummer breezes sway the fluffy white seed heads of cotton grasses. These may be found growing in the wetter parts of the bog, alongside reddish clumps of low-growing sundews.

Insect-eating plants

Three sundew species grow on British bogs: the great sundew, oblong-leaved sundew and round-leaved sundew, which is the most common. They all survive in the poor soil by trapping insects in their leaves.

Each leaf glistens with sticky, dewlike droplets borne on the ends of translucent red hairs. If an insect such as a fly lands on a leaf it sticks fast and the surrounding hairs curl inwards to trap it. The proteins in the insect's body are then digested by enzymes secreted from the centre of the leaf.

The harmless-looking butterworts also trap and eat insects. Their fleshy, slightly inward-rolled leaves are covered in a sticky secretion.

Blanket bogs, such as this one in the Forest of Bowland in Lancashire, may form where rainfall levels are high. A thick carpet of bog moss and deer grass is interspersed with dark pools.

DRAGONFLIES AND DAMSELFLIES

When summer sunshine raises the temperature, the air above bog pools becomes animated by dragonflies and damselflies. The larvae of a dozen or more species may live in the pools, where they hunt small animals.

Many peat bogs support a wide selection of these insects, with some rarer species restricted to certain regions. The busy four-spotted chaser and the black darter are both widespread and can be abundant. The former has distinctive wing spots, while the latter is a small, late summer species, the male of which is the only almost completely black dragonfly found in Britain. Male black darters start off with beautiful golden patches on their abdomens, but these fade as the black develops and spreads. Females are mainly a duller golden yellow and may be seen laying eggs in the peat around bog pools in August and September.

Northern bogs are graced by three rare specialities – the azure hawker and northern emerald, found only in Scotland, and the white-faced darter. The male azure hawker basks in the sunshine on exposed boulders, his long, blue-and-black body stretched out behind clear outspread wings. Once warmed up, he flies fast, skirting the pools in search of mates.

The other two species both appear very dark as they fly over the peaty water, but the northern emerald has bright green eyes, while the smaller, slender-bodied white-faced darter has a white 'face' and distinctive spots on its dark abdomen – red or orange in the male, yellow in the female. The chunkier and much more common four-spotted chaser also has a pale front to its head but this is not so white; its wing spots and size identify it.

The bogs of Wales and southern England have two specialities of their own. The delicate small red damselfly has a limited distribution, but where it occurs it can be plentiful. Fine weather lures out the brightly coloured

The black spots on its wings make the four-spotted chaser one of the most distinctive and easily recognised of the bog-loving dragonflies.

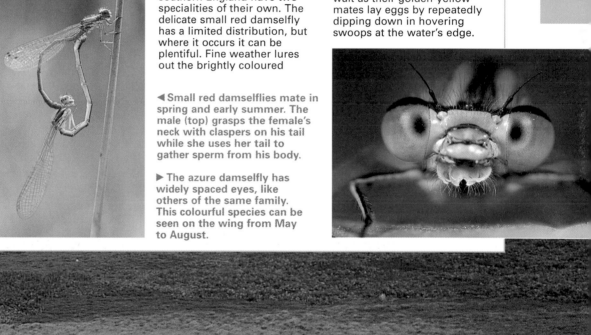

males and they head straight for the mossy breeding pools to pair with the darker females.

The keeled skimmer is more widespread. Pastel blue males rest on low perches, their wings drooping forwards, but soon fly up to chase off any approaching rivals. They often wait as their golden-yellow mates lay eggs by repeatedly dipping down in hovering swoops at the water's edge.

◀ **Small red damselflies mate in spring and early summer. The male (top) grasps the female's neck with claspers on his tail while she uses her tail to gather sperm from his body.**

▶ **The azure damselfly has widely spaced eyes, like others of the same family. This colourful species can be seen on the wing from May to August.**

Vivid yellow flowers of bog asphodel brighten up many peat bogs. The flower centres turn a deep orange as the fruit ripens at the end of summer.

An insect landing on the leaf is at first slowed down by the stickiness, then trapped as the leaf curls up over it. As with the sundews, leaf glands produce a fluid that digests the insect's body. Butterworts also digest fragments of plant material or pollen that fall on their leaves.

Summer flowers

In summer, both sundews and butterworts produce flowers on slender stems. The white flowers of sundews are tiny and inconspicuous, but butterwort flowers are more eyecatching, resembling those of violets. Other plants adding summer colour to the bog include the rather scarce marsh St John's wort and the much more widespread bog asphodel, with their fresh yellow petals. Luxuriant stands of bogbean emerge from bog pools, with shoots bearing large leaves in groups of three, and spikes of fluffy white flowers tinged with pink. A whole range of orchids may be seen, from the four species of tall, showy marsh orchids to the easily missed, diminutive bog orchid.

Dense thickets of bog myrtle may add a little vertical dimension to the habitat. This aromatic bush is best admired by scent rather than sight, as crushing a leaf releases a wonderful natural fragrance.

Bog pools

The mosses and other bog plants are punctuated by dark bog pools. The acidic, almost black waters look sterile, and indeed fish and wildfowl are mostly absent, but the palmate newt – Britain's smallest amphibian – is able to live in them and benefits from the absence of predatory company. In the breeding season the male palmate newt has partial blackish webbing on his hind toes, making his feet appear very big and dark.

Insects at the water's edge run the risk of being caught by a raft or swamp spider. This very large spider, the biggest found in Britain, has a velvet brown body with a pair of cream to pale orange stripes running its length. Despite its size it is light enough to be supported by the surface tension of the water, and it often lurks in wait for prey at the edge of a pool. It is fast and powerful enough to bring down prey much larger than itself, such as female dragonflies that come close to

Peculiar sounds can echo across lonely bogland. Sharp, snapping clicks emanating from the *Sphagnum* lawns are the unusual song of the large marsh grasshopper. One of the rarest grasshoppers, this boldly coloured insect is now restricted to the quaking bogs of Hampshire and Dorset, and parts of western Ireland. It is very wary, so a close view of its shiny yellow, black and green coloration requires a careful approach. If it feels threatened, the insect leaps across a pool to safety in a fleeting blur of colour.

The bog bush cricket is not quite as athletic as the grasshopper, but on warm days its repetitive chuffing song comes from within grassy tussocks. Bush crickets prefer to stay under cover, escaping from danger with rapid shuffling hops, unlike the longer bounds of the

Snipe breed on bogs, where their camouflage makes them hard to spot until they fly. Like many waders, their numbers have dropped sharply.

grasshopper. Bog bush crickets are often dull greyish-brown, but may be slightly more colourful with a shiny green cap.

A weird bleating noise from above the bog – neither frog nor sheep, yet strangely reminiscent of both – may herald the marvellous spectacle of a displaying male snipe. Circling overhead, the snipe climbs on rapid wing beats before dipping into successive shallow dives. He holds his stiff outer tail feathers at right angles, clear of the rest of his tail, to produce the bleating sound known as 'drumming'.

The large marsh grasshopper is the biggest grasshopper species in Britain. It inhabits wetlands, particularly areas where bog asphodel grows.

the water to lay their eggs. It may even dive below the surface to snatch tadpoles and small fish. After delivering a dose of paralysing poison with its fangs, the swamp spider moors its victim to the shore with a few hastily spun threads of silk before eating it.

Loose gangs of pond skaters also hunt over the water surface, using their needle-like mouthparts to inject poison into other insects that have landed on the water. The poison digests the tissues of their victims, allowing the pond skaters to suck them dry.

Sitting at the edge of a bog pool, supported by the water's surface tension, a swamp spider waits to feel vibrations through its sensitive feet, indicating a potential meal.

Unlike many of its showy relatives, the bog orchid is a tiny, delicate plant – the smallest orchid species in the British Isles. It grows among *Sphagnum* moss in the very wettest parts of bogs.

Pond skaters sometimes sport tiny red beads on their bodies, which on closer inspection turn out to be parasitic mites.

Bogland birds

Relatively few songbirds live on peat bogs, but wheatears, skylarks and meadow pipits find the isolation ideal for breeding. However, they can thrive only on pockets of dry land, and wheatears in particular, being hole-nesters, usually rely on stone walls and derelict bothies for breeding.

The main summer birds of peat bogs are nesting waders such as redshank, curlew and snipe. A bog speciality is the greenshank, which in mainland Britain breeds only on the vast peatlands of the Scottish Highlands. Like the other waders, it leaves at the end of summer to winter on coastal marshes and estuaries.

Land conservation

Many bogs have been almost destroyed by peat cutting, or even drained and planted with trees. One victim of this has been the Flow Country, a great expanse of bog that blankets much of Sutherland and Caithness in Scotland.

Although one of the most important boglands in the world, known for breeding birds that include red-throated and black-throated divers, the Flow Country has suffered because tax loopholes made it economically – if not environmentally – suitable for the planting of conifer trees. Vast tracts of land were drained and planted before conservationists managed to make the destruction an issue of national concern.

Thankfully, much of the planting has ceased, and huge tracts of the Flow Country remain unspoiled. Yet such threats emphasise the importance of preserving this rich, but fragile habitat.

Despite having suffered from tree planting in some parts, vast areas of Scotland's Flow Country have retained their pristine nature. Visitors can pick their way around the edges of this watery wilderness.

WILDLIFE WATCH

Where can I find peat bogs?

● Many areas of raised bog or valley mire are protected within Local or National Nature Reserves. They include Tregaron Bog and Borth Bog in Wales, Thursley Common in Surrey, Thorne Moors in South Yorkshire and the RSPB reserve at Arne in Dorset. National Nature Reserves include the Solway Mosses, Beinn Eighe in Wester Ross, and the Flow Country of Caithness and Sutherland. Some sites may have limited access or require a permit to enter. To contact English Nature for information, telephone 01733 455100 or visit www.english-nature.org.uk To contact the RSPB telephone 01767 680551 or visit www.rspb.org.uk

● Hill walkers may find their progress blocked by upland bogs, such as on the plateau top of Kinder Scout in the Peak District. These areas can look deceptively dry and firm from a distance, but may be dangerously impassable.

● To examine the wildlife of a less remote bog, visit your local common in summer and look out for the telltale yellow flowers of bog asphodel and fluffy seed heads of cotton-grasses. A few bogs exist in Greater London, for example on Wimbledon Common.

● The British Dragonfly Society has details of local activities. Contact The Secretary, British Dragonfly Society, The Haywain, Hollywater Road, Bordon, Hants GU35 0AD (telephone 01420 472329) or visit www.dragonflysoc.org.uk

● You could attempt to create a miniature bog habitat in your garden, to complement a garden pond or as a safer alternative for families with small children. Make sure you use only peat-free composts to help reduce the current high demand for peat, which is not sustainable.

Granite uplands

Rocky plateaus and outcrops, punctuated by a valley or two, combine to create some of Britain's most dramatic scenery. Alpine plants and lichens flower on sunnier slopes where upland berries such as cloudberry and bilberry slowly ripen.

Granite is one of the toughest of all rocks, and because of its erosion-resistant nature it forms the basis of many uplands. It dominates the geology of regions such as Dartmoor and Bodmin Moor in south-west England, and the summits of the Cairngorms and Ben Nevis in the Highlands of Scotland.

Originating in molten form deep beneath the Earth's surface, granite has been exposed by millions of years of erosion that have worn away the softer rocks above and around it. The process has left the granite as isolated outcrops and smoothed its rough edges to produce rounded hills and gentle valleys.

The slopes below high granite summits are littered with large boulders. Known as 'clitter' on Dartmoor, these provide sheltered spots for plants, and are often used by mammals and nesting birds. On the highest Scottish summits, frost-shattered boulders and thin gravel support the sparse plant community known as 'fell-field', which is typical of Arctic regions.

Although very hard, small fragments and granules do flake away from the surface of granite, preventing lichens from becoming established on exposed areas. Instead, the rock surfaces appear clean, and the fragments build up to form a thin, gravelly soil between the loose rocks, which may be colonised by upland plants.

Hard life

High altitude and exposure to harsh weather make survival in the uplands difficult for most plants. In regions where the underlying rock is soluble limestone, the soil often contains plant nutrients that have been dissolved from the rock by rainwater, and this helps. Granite, by contrast, is insoluble and impervious to water, so rainwater does not release any mineral nutrients from the rock. The water tends to collect above the rock, creating waterlogged conditions that prevent the breakdown of plant remains and limits the release of plant nutrients. Where the soil is more free-draining, high rainfall leaches out the few nutrients that do occur, leaving the soil acidic and impoverished.

Despite the poor soils, most uplands show signs of extensive human exploitation. Nine thousand years ago – when the upland climate seems to have been less harsh – many of these regions would have had dense tree cover. This has almost entirely vanished, partly due to climatic changes, but also through the clearance of trees for agriculture and intensive livestock grazing. The process began in the Neolithic period and has continued to the present day – grazing sheep on the moors still prevent the regeneration of woodland. So through a combination of natural and artificial factors, the ancient forests have been largely replaced by acidic grassland, heather moorland and peat bogs. Just a few fragments of forest remain to show how the uplands may have looked in the distant past.

Quarried cliffs

The tough, yet decorative nature of crystalline granite has made it useful for building, and many granite regions show evidence of centuries of quarrying. This has further diversified the habitats available, providing sheer rock faces, artificial scree slopes and deep pools in the bottoms of quarries.

Rarely straying far from the peaks, the ptarmigan has dense plumage – mottled in late summer – to combat the cold. Even its legs are protected by feathers.

▶ The granite mass of Ben Nevis is more than 500 million years old. The path to the summit provides good opportunities for watching wildlife.

DANGER!

Ben Nevis and the Cairngorms should not be tackled by unaccompanied inexperienced walkers, even in summer. Weather conditions can change rapidly and become very dangerous.

Woolly hair moss is found on frost-shattered granite uplands. It is often the only plant present on the highest peaks.

Small pools also appear on the surface of large granite outcrops. They look as if they are man-made, but are in fact formed by frost shattering the surface of the granite. They are never colonised by plants and aquatic animals because they dry out in summer and may freeze solid in winter.

Plant cover

The granite mass of Dartmoor lacks many of the alpine plant species associated with the granite mountains of Scotland. However, its high levels of rainfall have led to the development of blanket bogs. These extensive peatlands cover much of the higher part of the moor and support plants that are able to tolerate

and even thrive in the extreme environment. The dominant species on blanket bogs are various *Sphagnum* mosses, and when these die their remains are preserved by the acidic, waterlogged conditions to form deep layers of peat. Plant nutrients are extremely scarce, and some plants – butterworts, sundews and bladderworts – are adapted to gather extra nutrients by catching and digesting insects.

On the highest mountain tops, such as the summits of the Cairngorms, acidic grassland often gives way to open areas of small plants. These survive among the broken rocks that cover most of the summits. Mosses and lichens are the most common plants here, with a number of low-growing flowering plants that have a cushion-like form to help them withstand the harsh conditions. They

WHAT IS GRANITE?

Granite is a very hard rock that originated as hot fluid deep within the Earth's crust. This molten substance, or magma, consisted of a complex mixture of chemicals, which gradually cooled under enormous pressure as it moved towards the surface and eventually crystallised to create solid granite. The slower it cooled, the larger the crystals. Some granites contain crystals the size of wrapped sugar lumps.

The composition and final structure of each type of

granite vary according to the original chemical mix. Most granites consist of densely packed, randomly mixed crystals of quartz, feldspar and mica. The quartzes and feldspar are usually pale, but the mica forms small dark flecks. Most granites also contain small amounts of other minerals, such as iron pyrites or tourmaline, which add more colour to the rock.

Where the magma pushed up towards the surface, the heat partially melted the surrounding rocks, creating new minerals. This increases the diversity of the habitat, particularly on the fringes of the granite mass.

▲ **The individual crystals in granite are often easy to see, but a hand lens reveals their beauty. Their colour depends on the chemical ingredients.**

▶ **Granite masses are often divided by random cracks and joints. The crevices provide a precious roothold for tiny pioneering plants.**

A relative of the more familiar red campion of the lowlands, moss campion forms domed clumps which, for a brief period in summer, are covered with a mass of pink flowers.

include reindeer moss, *Cladonia rangifera*, which is actually a large, tufted lichen that grows in the gaps between loose rocks.

If the granite slopes or is unstable, slow-growing plants, such as mosses and lichens, are often unable to colonise successfully, but tougher plants, such as tufted hair grass, may be able to put down roots and form small clumps.

Flowering plants of high plateaus include moss campion and alpine lady's mantle, which is abundant on sunny slopes. Wetter areas where the granite has been replaced by lime-rich rocks are often brightened by yellow saxifrage. Cyphel, with its greenish flowers, is less conspicuous and the little pearlworts are even harder to find among the loose rocks. Starry saxifrage may grow in sheltered, wet areas and the highest Scottish peaks support the rare alpine, highland or tufted saxifrages.

Upland fruits

Despite the austerity of the environment, some hardy upland plants produce edible fruits in a good summer. Where a little more soil can accumulate, such as in the valleys and on gentler slopes, tough plants such as heathers are able to take root. Ling and bell heather are most common at high altitude, and in the north a variety of low, berry-bearing shrubs occur

▲ Dwarf cornel grows among the heather on drier areas of moorland. Its conspicuous midsummer blooms are followed by shiny red berries.

► Evergreen bearberry forms dense mats of woody stems on rocky slopes. It produces clusters of pink flowers followed by red edible berries in late summer.

▲ Trailing azalea is often found on bare mountain tops in the Cairngorms. Its tiny pink flowers and glossy leaves add colour to the high granite plateaus.

among them. Crowberry, with its shiny black berries, replaces the heathers on some slopes, while red-berried cowberry grows alongside bilberry – which has blue-black berries – on more sheltered slopes. Deciduous Arctic bearberry, which is found on Scottish moorland slopes, has shiny red berries. In early summer, wetter areas of moorland are dotted with the large white flowers of cloudberry. This low, creeping

In summer, herds of red deer move up on to the higher slopes to graze on the new shoots, but winters are spent down in the glens.

relative of the bramble is common on the slopes of the Cairngorms. Its white flowers are superseded by orange fruits in late summer.

Trees are almost entirely absent from the highest regions. Tall trees cannot survive, but a number of ground-hugging species can find a roothold where there is a little soil. In such places, the thin stems and small heart-shaped leaves of the least willow, *Salix herbacea*, can be found trailing over the ground. Like other willows, it produces catkins in early summer.

Summer visitors

The harsh climate, poor soils and limited plant growth make conditions very difficult for birds, mammals and invertebrates. Finding food is easy for a brief period in summer, when insect life is prolific and flowers and fruits are available, but for much of

the year, the high tops of moors and mountains are inhospitable places.

The diversity of insect life may be limited but in summer vast swarms of biting midges emerge from shallow peaty pools and make life miserable for warm-blooded animals. The mountain ringlet butterfly may be seen in grassy areas on calm days and lowland species, such as the small heath, sometimes flutter up to higher altitudes.

The insects attract a variety of birds, including snow buntings. In summer these live on Scotland's high peaks, nesting among boulders and feeding on insects and seeds. In autumn they migrate to lower altitudes where it is easier to find food. Ring ouzels are summer visitors from southern Europe that nest among rocks and on hillsides.

Many waders nest on the high plateaus in summer. Dotterel occur on the highest summits, nesting in open areas among the scattered rocks. These rare birds show an interesting role reversal, because the female is more boldly marked than the male and takes the lead in courtship; her mate incubates the eggs and rears the young. At the end of the season, dotterel leave the uplands and head for Africa.

Golden plovers are typical of these regions. Their nests are hidden in deep vegetation, but feeding birds may be seen on open grassland. In some boggy areas dunlins nest among the tussocks; these small waders arrive on the uplands in spring and announce their presence with trilling aerial displays. Both dunlins and golden plovers can be found nesting as far south as Dartmoor.

High granite uplands are also the home of ptarmigan, a hardy species of grouse. In summer, their white winter plumage is replaced by a mottled greyish-brown that allows the birds to blend in with the granite boulders.

Hunting birds

During the summer months, hen harriers and short-eared owls patrol the uplands in search of small birds and mammals. They join the resident buzzards and red kites, which are the largest birds of prey in southern Britain. In Scotland the magnificent golden eagle shares the remote uplands with ravens that nest on isolated outcrops and scavenge on the remains left by the hunters. Resident throughout the year, ravens build large nests that often have a warm lining of sheep's wool.

Few mammals can survive the difficult conditions of the high granite uplands. Grazing is poor, but there is usually enough to sustain the mountain hare. In Scotland, red deer wander up from the lowlands in summer to seek fresh growth, and in the Cairngorms an introduced herd of reindeer roam the highest areas where they feed on lichens and mosses.

The only large predatory mammal to hunt regularly in the uplands is the fox. In summer the boulder-strewn slopes provide foxes with ideal hiding places from which to hunt, but they retreat to the lowlands for the winter.

The spectacular golden eagle is the dominant avian predator of the northern granite uplands, where it hunts a variety of mammals and birds.

From a distance, weathered granite outcrops usually have a rounded appearance. Some of the best examples are the high tors of Dartmoor, such as Hound Tor, which is shown here.

In and around a dry-stone wall

What could seem more tranquil than a mossy limestone wall soaking up the summer sun? Yet its many cracks and crevices teem with a diverse selection of animal and plant life.

Although a dry-stone wall may look barren, its network of dark, dry, sheltered cavities provides an ideal place for a surprisingly large number of animals. It can be used both as a home and as a corridor through open upland landscapes.

On summer days a dry-stone wall absorbs the sun's warmth, storing it up and gradually releasing it through the night. This makes the wall a perfect refuge for small animals that lose heat easily – especially cold-blooded creatures, such as insects, which cannot generate their own warmth.

Butterfly suntraps
During the day the aptly named wall butterfly can often be seen flying along dry-stone walls and settling on the sun-warmed side. When the sun goes down, this butterfly simply nestles into the crevices to enjoy the storage-heater effect, along with other species, such as the small tortoiseshell and the painted lady.

Dry-stone walls built from limestone suit snails because they depend on limestone to provide the calcium for their shells. On damp nights and after rain the walls may be crawling with these gastropods coming out to look for food. One of the most impressive is the Roman snail, a spectacular cream-coloured species that performs extravagant mating rituals on damp summer evenings. The snails also provide succulent prey for carnivorous ground beetles that forage among the stones looking for a meal.

▼ Dry-stone walls are particularly useful to rabbits in areas of heavy or wet soils, which make burrows hard to dig and prone to flooding.

► The stoat's sinuous body allows it to streak in and out of a wall at high speed. Any rabbits, the stoat's main prey, are soon flushed out.

Basking reptiles

The warm stones are sought out by reptiles, such as the adder and slow-worm, which take refuge among the wall crevices. They also make use of places where a stretch of wall has fallen down, warming up in the morning by basking on the flat stones, or lying under them, camouflaged from predatory birds. In early summer they may be seen mating, but tread carefully and do not disturb them – adders may bite if stepped on and slow-worms may shed their tails if picked up.

Stony nurseries

Many dry-stone walls have formed field margins for hundreds of years, particularly in upland areas where plenty of stones are available. The walls are often fringed with trees, shrubs and bushes, such as elder, blackthorn and hawthorn. Along with rowan, dog rose and bramble, these trees bear berries that attract birds in late summer. Some birds, including pied wagtails, coal tits, spotted flycatchers, wrens and wheatears, may nest in the thorny tangles, or even among the stones of the walls.

The dark, hidden passages in walls sometimes attract rabbits. Usually, rabbits dig their own complex system of burrows, but a dry-stone wall can provide a sheltered nursery for their young. Here the baby rabbits can be born and raised until they are ready to forage on the field margin beside the wall. At any sign of danger they can dart back into their stony retreat.

The wall offers protection from enemies such as foxes, but it is no defence against the stoat. With its slim, flexible body and probing nature, this fierce, resourceful hunter is ideally equipped to comb the crevices for prey. So although the wall makes a good refuge, it can become a deadly trap.

▲ In treeless areas, short-eared owls and other hunting birds use walls as vantage points from which to survey fields for prey.

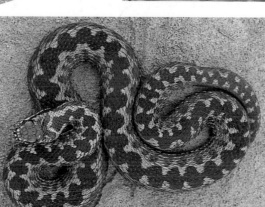

▲ The devil's coach-horse beetle is a distinctive inhabitant of the spaces in dry-stone walls. When alarmed, it raises its tail in an aggressive posture, at the same time emitting an offensive smell to deter attackers.

▶ For the adder, dry-stone walls offer sun-warmed stones to bask on and a supply of small mammals to eat.

▲ On a summer evening a search of a limestone wall may reveal a mating pair of snails. Shown here are Roman snails, an edible species thought to have been introduced by the Romans, which is probably the reason for their name.

Heaths – sandy suntraps

In late summer, heaths glow with the rich purple of flowering heather. Native ponies graze, reptiles bask in the sun and sometimes, on still evenings, the distinctive churring call of the nightjar fills the air.

The New Forest provides perhaps the most spectacular example of sandy, lowland heath, a much-diminished habitat, although some fine and extensive heathland can also be found in Suffolk, Sussex, Hampshire and Dorset. Similar heather-covered landscapes that occur in the uplands of the west and north owe their character to the high altitude and cool, wet climate. By contrast, the lower-lying heaths of southern Britain are warm and dry, and their vegetation reflects the acidic, infertile nature of their free-draining sandy or gravelly soils.

The growth and decline of open heath has been heavily influenced by the activities and attitudes of man. Although the soils of these regions have always been poor, they were originally colonised by trees such as birch, pine and even oak, which can tolerate relatively low-nutrient conditions. When the land began to be cleared for grazing, as long ago as the late Stone Age, it encouraged heather plants, which can thrive only on bare ground and are well adapted to acidic, impoverished soil. The heather seems to have taken over sandy or stony areas, and once it became established, grazing animals stopped the trees coming back by eating their seedlings. Animals may feed on heather, too, but this just encourages it to sprout new shoots.

Common land

Although good crops could not grow on heather, people of past centuries found many other uses for them, all of which served to keep the land clear of encroaching scrub. Heaths were often treated as

Bracken and heather share a 'pioneer' tactic whereby new growth sprouts rapidly from old roots and seeds, allowing both plants to colonise areas that have been burnt or cleared.

Reptiles such as this sand lizard are ectothermic, which means their body temperature is controlled by the temperature of their surroundings. A dry, open heath offers plenty of sunny spots where snakes and lizards can warm themselves.

'common land', on which farmers could graze their livestock as a 'commoner's right'. (This right still exists in some places, such as the New Forest.) The animals fed upon the grasses, heather shoots and any other foliage they could reach, and although the grazing was poor by most standards, their freedom to wander widely over the heath enabled them to find all the food they needed.

Natural resource
The heathland vegetation was also regularly gathered for other purposes. Heather and bracken were cut to provide bedding for both people and animals. The tough woody stems of heather made it useful for some construction purposes, such as path repairs, in thatching or as a material for making the wattle and daub panels used as infill on timber-framed buildings.

Along with birch saplings and the flexible stems of broom – a most aptly named plant – bunches of heather made effective yard brooms. Gorse and heather both burn readily and provided a useful domestic fuel.

All of these practices helped to maintain the heath by preventing the encroachment of trees and, as a result, these open spaces developed a rich diversity of specially adapted plants and animals.

Heathland was exploited in this way for many hundreds of years, but in the 19th century the spread of intensive farming and the decline of the common land system led to a change of attitude. The heaths came to be regarded as infertile, unproductive wastelands and many grazing and harvesting practices were

abandoned. With no discernible agricultural value, they became prime sites for development. Vast areas have been planted with conifer trees, which can grow in the poor soils, or quarried for their sand and gravel. Heaths have been used as sites for military airfields, housing developments and even nuclear power plants.

More natural, but equally damaging, has been the relentless spread of invasive pine and silver birch scrub that developed as heaths were neglected.

The dryness of heathlands, coupled with the flammable nature of the vegetation, makes them prone to wildfires. While these may encourage the heather – provided they do not burn too fiercely and destroy the seeds and root systems – they also encourage birch scrub, which destroys the heath habitat.

Fortunately, the wildlife and landscape value of heaths has now been recognised. Many surviving heaths have been designated protected wildlife reserves, where careful management, including

BIRDS OF OPEN HEATH

From early spring to well into summer the rich, prolonged, fluting notes of the woodlark pour down from above as the males display above the heath. They sail in circles on broad fluttering wings, singing all the while, then return to the ground. Here they are less easy to watch as they forage for food among the sparse grasses and young heather shoots.

Throughout early summer the heath is busy with the activity of breeding birds. Tree pipits – summer visitors from Africa – launch themselves from the tops of pine and birch trees, climb high in the air and then parachute down, emptying their lungs in a piping crescendo as they descend. On the more shrubby

parts of the heath the harsh scolding rasp of a Dartford warbler may be heard, although the bird can be hard to see as it lurks within the dense cover of gorse and heather. Occasionally, a male rewards a patient watcher with a better view when he flits up to perch on a sprig to render his thin, scratchy song, his red-rimmed eyes alert to danger. These residents are on the edge of their range in southern England, and suffer badly in hard winters.

▶ Dartford warblers may pair up for life. Both sexes share the tasks of incubating the eggs and feeding their young.

▶ The tree pipit is named for its habit of launching its song flight from a tree, rising into the air and drifting back down to a similar perch as it sings. The similar meadow pipit starts from the ground.

◀ The woodlark usually feeds on the ground, taking a variety of seeds and insects. It gathers a higher proportion of insects in the breeding season, because of their high protein content.

▼ A heathland specialist, the smooth snake feeds mainly on other reptiles. It is not venomous – it simply seizes its prey, coils around it, then swallows it alive, head-first.

▲ It takes a slow, stealthy approach to get this close to an adder. They are wary creatures, and most people glimpse only a tail tip slipping into the heather.

◄ Grass snakes may be found on the wetter parts of the heath, where they are more likely to come across their favourite prey – frogs and newts.

controlled grazing by horses, cattle and sheep, allows the distinctive plant and animal life to prosper.

Heathland life

At low level the heath is alive with small animals. Black ants gather food among the scattered heather litter and moss cushions, funnel-weaving spiders skulk in the recesses of their nests spun among low-growing plants, while tiny grey flasks made of mud attached to heather stalks show that potter wasps have been busy making nurseries for their larvae. Meanwhile, the energetic reeling and chirping of grasshoppers and bush crickets fills the air.

Some of these insects are targeted by the green tiger beetle, a lone hunter no bigger than a thumbnail, that can often be seen springing across open sand. Not an easy insect to approach, it explodes into buzzing flight when it feels threatened, landing a short way off. A close view is worth the effort, however, since it is a handsome insect with beautiful metallic green wing cases dotted with yellow, and sharp, oversized jaws.

From the middle of June into September a succession of flowers make the heath glow with colour. Yellow gorse and broom complement the purples and pinks of the heathers, and nectar-hungry bees work tirelessly to make the most of the season. Day-flying moths flit low across the heathers – some pause to sip nectar while others, such as the sturdy brown fox moth, tend to fly directly across the heath apparently without stopping. Colourful species, such as the clouded buff moth and emperor moth, are outnumbered by the common heath moth, a small, speckled brownish moth that often falls prey to aerial hunters, such as the black-tailed skimmer dragonfly.

Many butterflies visit to feast on the nectar, and a few – such as the grayling and silver-studded blue – are specialists

HEATHLAND HOPPERS

Heaths are good habitats for grasshoppers and crickets. To tell the difference between them, look at their antennae. A grasshopper has short antennae, while those of a cricket are long and whippy, and swept back over the insect's body. Crickets are less inclined to leap.

Two heathland specialists are the chunky bog bush cricket and the tiny mottled grasshopper. Get down close and watch as they sing – the bush cricket flicks its stumpy wing scales (useless for flying) across each other to produce a soft repetitive grating, while the mottled grasshopper makes its whirring buzz by rubbing its legs up and down across its folded wings. The mottled grasshopper can also use its wings to extend its leaps into short flights over the heather. Both insects are most active from early summer until the nights get cold in autumn.

► The buzzing of the mottled grasshopper is a common sound of summer heathland, where the insect feeds on a variety of grasses and other plants. Its big eyes give it virtually all-round vision.

◄ Wetter parts of the heath are home to the bog bush cricket. It is common on moorland in many areas of England and Wales.

that depend on heathland throughout their life cycle. The caterpillars of the silver-studded blue, for example, feed on young heather and gorse. Adults can be seen on the wing during high summer, feeding from the nectar-laden blooms of bell heather.

Male silver-studded blues can be approached as they sunbathe. Their darker blue upper wings are edged with broad black margins which help to distinguish them from the brighter common blues that wander onto heaths. Females are smaller and have velvety brown wings with orange markings towards the rear of their hind wings. The silver studs that give this butterfly its name can be seen – but only just – in the middle of some of the dark spots bordering the underwing when the butterfly folds its wings over its back.

The grayling is a larger butterfly, but much harder to see when it is not moving. Its mottled brown underwings make for perfect camouflage

Grazing and trampling – by ponies, for instance – is the secret of maintaining a good heathland habitat. It prevents the growth of trees, which would overshadow the heather and lower the soil temperatures.

as it rests on the stony or sandy ground among the heather litter. On cool days it has a habit of warming up by leaning over to one side, with its wings closed to present them square on to the sun, and so absorb more heat.

Sand diggers
The sand digger wasp never seems able to decide whether to run or fly as it searches for its burrow entrance in the sand. Quite unlike the common wasps, it has a broad black head with bulging eyes, and a slender black and orange waist ending in a swollen orange and black tail.

Its tunnel entrance holes are easy to spot on the open ground or on sunny sand banks, and provide warm incubators for its larvae. It stocks the burrow with caterpillars that it paralyses with its sting, and the helpless insects remain alive as they are devoured by the wasp's hungry larvae.

Many other insects burrow in the sand and some leave telltale evidence of their digging. Solitary mining bees, for example, heap cones of sand grains around their excavations, creating a site that resembles a miniature crater-field on the moon.

▲ **Large eyes give the nightjar sensitive vision, which it uses to hunt flying insects at dusk. Each pair of birds may raise two broods of two young during a single breeding season.**

◀ **Fire can encourage heather, but if fires are too frequent they can cause the region to become dominated by other species, including grasses, gorse and fast-growing silver birch trees.**

Life proceeds at a more sedate pace for the minotaur beetle. The shiny black males have elaborately sculptured thoraxes sporting three long forward-facing horns, while females have a similar arrangement of short knobs. They are dung beetles that specialise in collecting the droppings of the rabbits and sheep that graze the heath, and either eating them or burying them as food stores for their young.

Reptile haven
Reptiles generally thrive on dry heathland and the finest Dorset heaths still support all six native British snakes and lizards. Of these, the common lizard, slow-worm, adder and grass snake are common heathland species, but the sand lizard and the secretive, well-camouflaged smooth snake are now rare. The magnificent sand lizard,

in particular, has suffered serious declines on southern heaths, but is now being carefully conserved.

In the breeding season the male sports flashy green flanks to attract a mate, while the female has a browner pattern that helps to conceal her from airborne predators, such as kestrels and crows. Her scales are marked with an intricate spotted pattern that breaks up her outline as she moves among the heather stems. In early summer she digs a burrow for her eggs, which need to be kept warm, safe from flooding and away from the trampling feet of people and ponies. Sloping banks of sandy heath with a southerly aspect are ideal.

The smooth snake has a similar distribution on southern heathland, where it feeds mainly upon other reptiles and is a major predator of the rare sand lizard. The smooth snake spends much of its time either underground or resting beneath warm stones, and is hard to find even on heathland where it is relatively numerous.

Noises in the night

On warm summer evenings, when biting midges swarm up from the heathland bracken, the nightjar fills the gathering dusk with its weird churring song. Rising and falling in intensity, the male's churring can drone on for extended periods, but the calling bird may be difficult to locate in the twilight – he may be

perched along a pine branch, squatting low on a stump or just sitting on the ground. Even by daylight the nightjar's mottled, subtly beautiful camouflage makes the bird virtually invisible against tree bark.

Liquid 'cu-ik' calls and clapping sounds – made by the male nightjar flapping his wings together – indicate that the bird has flown. On still, warm evenings a careful watcher may be rewarded by the sight of a slender falcon-like shape floating and gliding over the heather with a lazy dancing flight, as the nightjar hunts for airborne evening insects, such as moths and flying beetles. As darkness falls over the heath the bird vanishes, leaving the summer night air to the bats and owls.

▲ The green tiger beetle is a handsome, swift hunter. It also flies briskly, in short bursts, across the heath in search of prey – or to avoid possible danger.

HEATHLAND PLANTS

The heathland plant seen most often is ling, a hardy species of heather that thrives in poor sandy, gravelly or peaty soils and forms the basis of the heath ecosystem. It can tolerate grazing, cutting and burning, and its seeds can lie dormant for years before germinating when conditions suit. If ling is left

▼ Bright yellow gorse flowers are highly attractive to several bee species that live on heathland. Dried gorse burns well and used to be gathered for fuel.

unmanaged, it can grow into woody bushes up to 1.5m (5ft) tall before the leggy stems die back and collapse to allow space for fresh young growth.

Late summer spikes of delicate pinkish flowers distinguish ling from the deeper purplish flowers of bell heather, which often grows among ling on drier sites. Bell heather leaves are waxy, bronze-green needles, giving the stems a spiny appearance; ling has tiny scale-like grey-green leaves.

On wetter sites, ling is partnered by more conspicuous,

▶ The leaves of cross-leaved heath grow in sets of four, forming crosses at intervals along the stems. The flowers are rose-pink.

pink-flowered cross-leaved heath. Rarer Dorset and Cornish heaths occur in a few areas only.

For much of the year, the golden flowers of broom and gorse provide a dramatic contrast to the pink and purple heathers. Of the three species of gorse, common and western gorse are widespread, but dwarf gorse occurs mainly in the south-east.

▲ Broom resembles flowering gorse but its distinctive green stems are not prickly. Both broom and gorse produce dark seed pods.

◀ Bell heather (on right) and ling are to be found on most heaths.

The female sand digger wasp uses her sting to paralyse a caterpillar, which she bundles into a nursery burrow. She lays an egg on top and seals the entrance. When the egg hatches, the still-living caterpillar becomes food for the wasp grub.

Heathlands occur on sandy soils and are dominated by heathers. Gorse and other shrubs add diversity, but if these become dominant they cast shade, reducing the quality of the area for heather, insects and other heathland wildlife.

WILDLIFE WATCH

Where can I explore heaths?

● Visit a heath in spring or early summer to enjoy the birds, or in late summer for the insects and the purple carpet of heather.

● Go on an organised nightjar watch – contact your nearest heathland reserve warden to find out what is arranged.

● Reptile watching is never easy – get your eye in by visiting the New Forest reptiliary near Holidays Hill on the A35. Here you can see all Britain's native snakes and lizards in natural settings.

● Visit Thursley Common in Surrey to watch the lizards on the wooden boardwalks, and enjoy the dragonflies. Choose a sunny day for any reptile-watching expedition.

● Contact English Nature for details of 'Tomorrow's Heathland Heritage' – a project designed to conserve heaths. Telephone 01733 455100 or visit www.english-nature.org.uk/thh

● Help out at a heathland conservation work party with the local wildlife trust – great fun and very worthwhile.

● Fine examples of heaths can be found at: Dunwich Heath and North Warren RSPB Reserve in Suffolk; Chobham, Frensham and Thursley Commons in Surrey; Wildmoor Heath in Berkshire; Ashdown Forest in East Sussex; the New Forest in Hampshire and Dorset; Godlingston, Canford and Studland Heaths and Arne RSPB Reserve in Dorset.

▲ The clouded buff is a species of heathland tiger moth. It lays its eggs on heather.

◀ The grayling butterfly performs a disappearing act simply by settling on a sandy patch and folding its wings: only the sand-coloured parts can then be seen.

The Peak District – land of hill and dale

From rugged moorland in the north to gentler meadows in the south, this is a region of conspicuous contrasts. In early summer, the crags and cliffs, woods and valleys come alive with birdsong and brightly coloured flowers.

The Peak District lies at the junction of highland and lowland Britain, at the southern tip of the Pennines. For this reason it contains an impressive variety of wildlife habitats, from the bleak moors of the northern region to the softer meadows and dales of the south. It has been popular with visitors since the 19th century, when the beauty of wild, rugged landscape was celebrated by writers and painters. Surrounded by the great industrial cities of England, the area was a natural leisure destination for thousands of people. It was not until 1951, however, that the Peak District was designated a National Park, Britain's first. It now covers some 1500 square kilometres (560 square miles).

Diverging landscape

The two distinct areas of the region are known as the Dark Peak and the White Peak, the former taking its name from the prevalent gritstone moors. The Dark Peak surrounds the southern white limestone,

Ling, the common heather, adds a splash of colour to the bleak moorlands. Derwent Edge (below) is at its most splendid in July and August when the ling is in bloom.

which forms the White Peak, like a horseshoe. Fringed with steep cliffs and weirdly weathered tors, it includes the highest, wildest land in the park, rising to 636m (2087ft) above sea level on the flat, desolate top of Kinder Scout. The names of the other major hills, Bleaklow and Black Hill, provide a clue to their uncompromising nature, and they mark the first stage of Britain's toughest long-distance footpath, the 430km (267 mile) Pennine Way.

Peat bogs developed on the high plateaus during periods of heavy rainfall, particularly from around 600 BC. The *Sphagnum* (bog moss) has gone – probably killed by pollution during the Industrial Revolution – and common cotton-grass, a type of sedge, has taken its place. A few areas also have cloudberry, a dwarf blackberry with orange fruits.

As the peat dries it is eroded by the wind, forming dramatic patterns across this wild tableland. Gullies crisscross the landscape cutting deep into the peat, revealing the

Mountain hares have been introduced to the Peak District. In spring they moult their white winter fur to reveal a grey-brown summer coat that matches the colours of the moors.

◄ A close relative of the blackbird, the ring ouzel arrives in spring to breed in the remote uplands. Although timid, the males may perch in the open to sing.

► The bouncy, ground-loving wheatear returns from Africa to breed in March. Despite its pale underparts, the male wheatear is well camouflaged and hard to see among the upland rocks.

The red grouse is a familiar sight on the Peak District moorlands. Some areas are specially managed for the species. Rarely seen out in the open, red grouse will take to the wing if disturbed, flying low over the heather.

glittering millstone gravels beneath and leaving a mosaic of long, dark hummocky banks of peat, known as hags. Hare's-tail cotton-grass, crowberry and bilberry grow here, and dunlin, golden plover and curlew nest among the low vegetation.

Below the plateau, heather and bilberry carpet the slopes where the peat is thinner,

Natural rock formations known as the Wheel Stones, on Derwent Edge near Barnford, are among the most evocative geological formations of the Dark Peak.

giving way to spreads of mat-grass and purple moor-grass. These areas have been grazed by sheep for centuries, and local sheep breeds such as the Derbyshire gritstone are famed for their hardiness.

Grouse moors

The heather moors are a distinctive part of the Peak District landscape, yet 4000 years ago most of today's moorland would have been wild woodlands. They were initially cleared to make way for stock and only in the last century were the moors specially managed for grouse. Their distinctive 'go-back, go-back, go-back, back, back' calls are part of the character of the uplands, but they fall silent when hunting peregrines appear overhead. The little

merlin takes smaller quarry, such as meadow pipits and skylarks. In winter these birds of prey are joined by hen harriers and short-eared owls.

Throughout summer the moors ring to the evocative calls of curlew and golden plover. The curlews rise high into the sky and hold their wings still as they glide back down, uttering their beautiful bubbling song. Snipe and dunlin also breed in this wild, barren landscape. In the rocky 'cloughs' the strident call of the ring ouzel – or 'mountain blackbird' – can be heard.

Gradual deforestation has robbed the high ground of the native sessile oak woods

► Dark, blue-black berries of bilberry, often hidden by other moorland vegetation, are sought out by a variety of birds.

that would have once covered much of the Dark Peak. Grazing has prevented regeneration in most areas, but on some slopes twisted, stunted oaks still cling to the rocky hillsides, along with rowan and silver birch.

The damp woodlands just to the north of Ladybower Reservoir are superb for mosses, lichens and liverworts.

◄ The bulbous fruits of the cloudberry are born by the female plant and are rarely seen because male flowers tend to predominate. In Britain, this subalpine shrub is found only on moorland.

MAN-MADE HABITATS

The moors of the Dark Peak end abruptly in short, steep escarpments of naked rock, known locally as 'edges', which frown down on the valleys. Some 50 of these Dark Peak valleys have been flooded to create reservoirs, providing much-needed supplies of fresh water to the surrounding ring of industrial cities and towns. Those that fill the Upper Derwent Valley, such as the Howden, Derwent and Ladybower reservoirs, are ringed with belts of dense conifer plantations.

While these areas of the park are entirely artificial, they add an extra dimension to the patchwork of habitats that is such a feature of the region. It is here that the goshawk – a bigger, more rare cousin of the sparrowhawk – may be seen displaying over the trees during the breeding season. Crossbills feed on pine cones, carefully removing the seeds with their unique, twisted bills, and coal tits and goldcrests flit through the trees in mixed flocks. Goosanders and red-breasted mergansers fish in the acidic water of the reservoirs, and common sandpipers search for food along the shore, uttering shrill, piping three-note calls as they fly off on flicking, stiffly bowed wings.

◄ Crossbills may be seen feeding high in the branches of pine and larch trees that are mature enough to bear cones. This is a male – the female has green plumage.

▶ Red-breasted merganser breed in the Peak District in small numbers, making their nests on the ground near reservoirs. This is a male bird.

The acidic soil, however, does not encourage the profusion of wild flowers that is such a feature of the limestone dales further south. Instead, bilberry, cowberry, bracken and heather dominate.

By early summer these woods ring with the songs of redstarts, willow warblers and tree pipits, as well as the distinctive call of the cuckoo. Kestrels hover on the updraughts above the cliffs and find ideal nesting sites in the crags, along with jackdaws and occasional ravens.

Limestone dales

The frowning rocks of the Dark Peak give way to the White Peak, a land of seemingly endless limestone drystone walls. These climb up hill and down dale like a huge net, holding down the billowing emerald-green pastures. The walls are so much part of the landscape that they seem to grow naturally out of the ground. In fact, they were created during the land enclosure movement of the 18th and 19th centuries. They now provide havens for stoats, weasels, mice and voles, as well as the wheatears and stonechats that flit along their tops, scolding as they go.

The White Peak takes its name from the pale limestone that was laid down during the Carboniferous period around 350 million years ago, when the area was covered with a warm sea that was rich in animal life. A close look at a gatepost or stile will often reveal the fossilised remains of tiny sea creatures, the skeletons of which built up to form the limestone.

The precipitous, crag-lined dales that split this limestone plateau were formed by the erosive action of melt water from Ice Age glaciers, which departed the scene only around 10,000 years ago. They also helped, along with the acidic action of rainwater, to form the extensive cave systems that underlie many

The view from Derwent Edge towards Edale encompasses a range of Peak District scenery, from conifer plantations and walled pastures to heather-clad high moorlands.

▲ The green hairstreak's brightly coloured underwings provide excellent camouflage, perfectly matching the leaves on which they rest.

◄ Short-eared owls often hunt by day, favouring areas of short grassland.

of the limestone areas of the Peak District, such as in the Castleton area of the Hope Valley, where several caverns are open to visitors.

A feral population of red-necked wallabies lives in the area, much to the bemusement of walkers who may encounter them on Kinder Scout and on the moors in the south-west of the park. The wallabies' ancestors escaped from a private menagerie in Swythamley Park in Staffordshire in about 1940.

Flower-rich hills

The short grassland of the limestone hills and dales are noted for their flowers. For people living in the south, this is the nearest place where

some of Britain's more northerly species can be seen, such as the particularly lovely Jacob's-ladder with its spires of bright purplish blue flowers. The name is probably derived from the leaves, which are made up of rows of rung-like leaflets. The globeflower is another speciality; it has striking butter-yellow petals tightly bunched together like those of old-fashioned roses.

In more open areas, cowslips and early purple orchids are the most noticeable early flowering species. As the weeks go by, the grassland becomes increasingly flower-filled with bird's-foot trefoil, harebell and burnet saxifrage, followed later in the year by the purple

flowers of devil's-bit scabious and the delicate white petals of grass-of-Parnassus.

Some plants, such as wall-pepper, have fleshy, water-storing leaves so they can survive the drought conditions of the south-facing rocky outcrops. Others, such as salad burnet, have long roots that grow deeply into the cracks.

In shady woodland areas the rare, scented shrub, mezereon, and its more common relative, spurge-laurel, flower early along with the occasional yellow star-of-Bethlehem. Later, the sharp-eyed may spot herb-Paris disguised among the carpets of dog's mercury. No one can miss the heavy scent of lily-of-the-valley or the tall

nettle-leaved bellflower with its glorious purple-blue bell-shaped flowers.

Most of the limestone grassland has been reseeded with high-yielding grasses for grazing animals, but the few 'unimproved' fields that remain are bejewelled with ox-eye daisy and yellow-rattle. Meadow crane's-bill, knapweed and numerous other flowers enliven the roadside verges, where they escape grazing or cutting.

Today, the only truly natural landscape in the White Peak is on the steep, rocky sides of the dales, many of which are protected as nature reserves

▶ The inquisitive stoat roams the northern moorland, where rocky outcrops provide ideal crevices for dens.

◄ Small by the standards of most ferns, green spleenwort anchors itself in shady niches in exposed crags and walls.

▲ The yellow star-of-Bethlehem adorns the woodland floor in a few places where ash is the predominant tree species.

▲ Beautiful purple spires of Jacob's-ladder may be a familiar sight in gardens, but the plant grows wild only on the limestone soils of Lathkill Dale in the Peak District.

▲ Tolerant of soils laden with lead and other metals, spring sandwort is often a sign of a long history of lead mining in the area.

DANGER!

The weather can change dramatically in the Peaks, so be prepared. Always carry a map and compass, bad-weather clothing and emergency rations, and tell someone where you are going.

Drifts of tassel-headed cotton grass are a good indication that the ground below is boggy and dangerous.

because of their wealth of wildlife. Perhaps most famous is Dovedale, north of Ashbourne, now protected by the National Trust, which has echoed to the praises of visitors since the mid-17th century. The crystal-clear waters of these pure streams hold a variety of insect life that is sensitive to pollution, such as mayfly, caddisfly and stonefly larvae. They are preyed upon by dippers that can swim under the water, while grey wagtails snatch the adult insects in flight.

The natural woodland of the White Peak is ash, with an understorey of hazel, guelder rose and bird cherry. Green woodpeckers, treecreepers and nuthatches are among the year-round residents, with migrant redstarts, blackcaps and willow warblers swelling the numbers in the summer.

Cliff woodlands

Some woodlands manage to grow on the limestone cliffs, where rock whitebeam and yew cling on above long curtains of mountain currant. Shady cracks filled with soil are home to ferns such as rustyback, green spleenwort, brittle bladder-fern and the rare limestone oak fern.

Nature has taken over the old limestone quarries that were worked until the 1930s. The stone was mined and burnt in kilns to transform it to quicklime, which was used

Feral populations of red-necked wallabies roam parts of the Peak District. Unlike many other alien species, the wallabies do not appear to have damaged the native flora.

by hill farmers to improve the grazing pasture on acid moorland. The heaps of waste stone have been colonised by cowslips, lady's mantle, harebell and wild strawberry.

The tiny, wind-blown seeds of fragrant and bee orchids have settled and established themselves on the bare quarry floors. Colonies of wild flowers such as eyebright, thyme and bird's-foot trefoil, the foodplant of the common blue butterfly, also manage to grow on the thin soils.

Wherever there is a good variety of flowers, insects will follow. On sunny days green hairstreaks and skipper

butterflies can be seen, as well as brown argus – which is at the southern limit of its range here – and the day-flying six-spot burnet moth.

Lead mining was an important part of the local economy from Roman times, and in the first half of the 18th century, up to 10,000 miners worked the lead rakes and veins that crisscross the White Peak. Now deserted, these mines have developed their own rich plant life. Spring sandwort or leadwort, with its tiny white flowers, is tolerant of the toxic soil close to the mines. Bright yellow flowers of mountain pansy bloom in places where the soil is slightly acidic, and a close inspection may reveal moonwort, a strange little fern that copes well with the high levels of lead in the soil.

Places to visit in the Peak District

The National Park extends from south of Huddersfield in the north to Ashbourne in the south, and lies on the doorsteps of Manchester, Sheffield and Stoke-on-Trent. The moorland of the Dark Peak offers open access, whereas the White Peak is more intensively farmed and visitors must follow the trails and footpaths provided. The following are some good places to see wildlife.

1 Kinder Scout
Kinder Scout is the highest point of the Peak District and the views from the summit are superb. It is part of the High Peak estate, belonging to the National Trust, which also includes the Hope Woodlands. These are, in fact, mostly moorland. To the south is the Longshaw Estate, where a visitor centre provides information about the Trust's large land holdings in the Peak District. All offer fine walking with dramatic views.

2 The Derbyshire Dales National Nature Reserve
This region of 325 hectares (800 acres) consists of five of the best dales – Lathkill Dale, Monk's Dale, Cressbrook Dale, Biggin Dale and Long Dale. It contains some of the finest scenery and wildlife in the area and is managed by English Nature. If you are interested in wild flowers, walk up either Lathkill Dale or Monk's Dale to enjoy a fine variety of limestone species.

3–5 The Monsal, Tissington and the High Peak Trails
These all follow former railway lines. Leaflets are available from the National Park information centres. The Monsal Trail (3) passes three Derbyshire Wildlife Trust reserves – Millers Dale Quarry, a disused limestone quarry, Priestcliffe Lees, an old lead workings, and Chee Dale, a fine limestone dale with cliff-nesting house martins. Where the trail follows the River Wye, look out for dipper, grey wagtail and, if you are lucky, the blue flash of a kingfisher. The Tissington Trail (4) runs from Ashbourne to Buxton and High Peak Trail (5) meets it at Parsley Hay. They are fairly wooded with a good range of breeding woodland birds, including wood warblers and redstarts.

6 The Derwent Valley
The reservoirs of the Derwent Valley, of which Ladybower is the largest, are well worth checking for red-breasted merganser, common sandpiper and little ringed plover in summer. At the beginning and end of the season there is the chance of spotting a fishing osprey. Later in the year, look out for winter wildfowl including pochard, goldeneye and goosander.

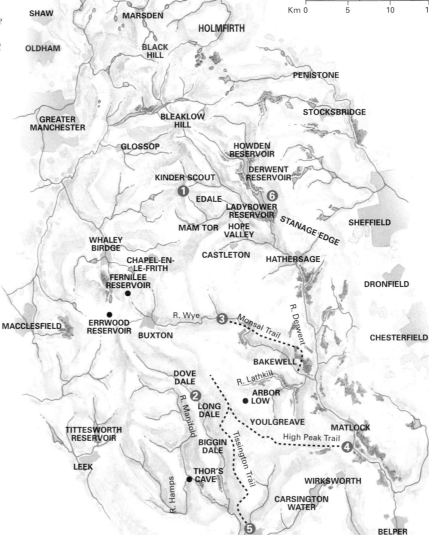

WILDLIFE WATCH

When can I see wildlife in the Peak District?

● Late May to July is the best time to look for the flowers of the Dales, although mezereon and yellow star-of-Bethlehem bloom as early as March. For the special flowers of the old quarries and lead workings visit one of the nature reserves.

● In June, the summer migrants return to the Peaks and the woods are filled with the singing of warblers such as the wood warbler, as well as the drumming of the resident woodpecker. Earlier, in the spring, the breeding birds display. On warm days look out for goshawks spiralling high over the conifer plantations.

● The high moors are exhilarating for walking at any time of year, with the chance of seeing hen harriers, short-eared owls and the odd mountain hare.

Eroded over time by rainwater, the limestone of the Peak District has formed underground caverns with some magnificent stalactites and stalagmites.

Animals and plants in focus

Moorland watch

- Native ponies
- The pine marten
- The kestrel
- The cuckoo
- The hobby
- The adder
- Recognising moorland butterflies
- Heaths and heathers
- Moorland grasses

Native ponies

Today's descendants of old wild herds search out lush pasture throughout the summer months. Unshod and ungroomed, these robust animals wander freely but survive only with the help of human intervention.

Thousands of years ago, truly wild horses and ponies colonised the land but, over the centuries, these creatures became extinct and various present-day breeds, such as those found on Exmoor and in the New Forest, have taken their place. The Exmoor pony is probably the closest surviving relative of the ancient stock, although the wild ponies that inhabit the New Forest in Hampshire have been present since Saxon times.

Today, native pony herds are managed by humans. New blood from domestic stock has been introduced over the years to improve the commercial value of the herds, so most native ponies in the British Isles are now mixed in terms of their genes.

The strict definition of a pony is based on height at the shoulder – under 14.2 hands, or 1.47m (4ft 10in) – and on build. Compared to horses, ponies tend to be stockier, with shorter legs in proportion to their bodies, which means they take shorter strides. Pony foals are not so gangly looking as horse foals.

Although they roam freely across the open hills and moors, all of Britain's native ponies belong to someone. Those in the New Forest are owned by local people who hold commoner's rights to graze them on open land in the forest. New Forest and Exmoor ponies are rounded up every autumn to establish ownership and to check on the animals' welfare. Weak and sick ponies receive veterinary treatment and, if the herd is growing too large to be sustainable, any surplus animals are removed and sold.

Grazing animals

Grass forms more than three-quarters of the summer diet of native ponies. With muscular jaws and large, square-crowned teeth that grow throughout their lives to compensate for being worn away by the tough food, they are adapted to eating large quantities of it. However, ponies are less effective than cows at digesting grass, which is why pony droppings are fibrous, containing a high proportion of matter that has not been completely digested.

ANCIENT BREED

The ancestor of the domestic horse – and hence ponies – is thought to be Przewalski's horse of Asia. The true wild horses that lived in Britain in the company of woolly mammoths at the end of the last Ice Age were probably akin to this species. They died out about 9500 years ago as the climate improved, habitat was lost and the herds came under pressure from early humans. Later, they were replaced by domestic horses imported during the Iron Age.

It is possible, but unlikely, that Exmoor ponies are direct descendants of the original wild horses. It is more probable that they are a mixture of wild and domestic stock that has roamed freely for thousands of years – they are certainly the most ancient of the various types of wild pony found in Britain and Ireland. Only about 180 purebred Exmoors are left on the 17,000 hectares (42,000 acres) of Exmoor moorland and they are accompanied by increasing numbers of crossbred animals.

Stocky Dartmoor ponies are probably descended from Exmoors and are perfectly adapted to survival on steep, rock-strewn slopes. Wild ponies have lived on Dartmoor for at least a thousand years.

NATIVE PONY FACT FILE

Ten native breeds of pony live on mountains and moorland in the British Isles, and in the ancient hunting grounds of the New Forest. Many different colours and markings are found in the different breeds as a result of their diverse heritage.

● NAMES
Common names: Dartmoor pony, Exmoor pony, New Forest pony, Dales pony, Fell pony, Highland pony, Eriskay pony, Shetland pony, Welsh Mountain pony, Connemara pony
Scientific name: *Equus caballus*

● HABITAT
Moorland, mountains and forest

● DISTRIBUTION
Semi-wild herds in Dartmoor, Exmoor, New Forest, Welsh mountains, both sides of Pennines, Scottish Highlands and Islands, Shetland Isles and Connemara in County Galway, Ireland

● STATUS
Pure breeds nationally scarce, but often abundant in their native areas

● SIZE
Height at shoulder: varies from Shetland pony at about 1m (3ft) to Connemara, Dales and Highland ponies up to about 1.47m (4ft 10in)

● KEY FEATURES
Sturdy and strong, with deep chest and short, strong legs; variably coloured according to breed; coat appears fine and glossy in summer, dense and hairy in winter; long tail and mane

● HABITS
Sociable, living in small herds; not afraid of people or cars; active day and night

● VOICE
Horse-like whinny (or neigh) and snorts

● FOOD
Mainly grass; heather, moss, leaves, holly and shrubs, such as gorse and bramble, in winter

● BREEDING
Mating occurs in summer; gestation averages 335 days and foals are born in the open March–September (occasionally later) the following year, most born April–May

● YOUNG
Resemble adult

● SIGNS
Large heaps of coarse, round faecal pellets (or droppings), each ball about 5cm (2in) in diameter; footprints semi-circular

There is no restriction on the breed of stallion that can be turned out on Dartmoor, so today few of the ponies in the area are pure-bred. Grey and chestnut foals are not unusual.

Distribution map key

■	Present
□	Not present

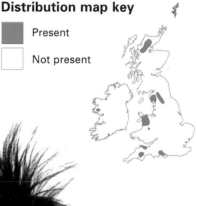

Colour varies from black and brown to chestnut and grey.

Some ponies are branded to establish ownership.

The mane and forelock are usually long, thick and shaggy.

Most native ponies have a thick neck supporting a heavy head.

Some breeds have 'feathers', or long hair, on the lower leg.

Strong legs and tough hooves are common to all native breeds.

SHETLAND PONY – ISLAND DWELLER

Shetland ponies originate from the wild, open islands to the north of the Scottish mainland. Nowhere is far from the sea, and the islands are lashed by wind and rain, even in summer. There is little shelter in this treeless landscape, so the ponies must be robust and hardy. The soils are poor and support grass that is not very nourishing – some of the ponies even visit the shore to eat seaweed.

Perhaps due to their relatively impoverished diet, Shetland ponies did not develop into large animals and, as a result, are a miniature breed. Another theory is that they are descended from dwarf ponies similar to Exmoors.

Ponies were brought to Shetland perhaps as

much as a thousand years ago to assist in settling the islands. By about 1800, they were being exported back to the mainland as mounts for children. In 1847, child labour was abolished in British coal mines and suddenly there was a great demand for tiny Shetland ponies to replace them, pulling carts of coal in the cramped underground conditions. The effect was to reduce the pony population on the islands by half, from a maximum of about 10,000.

The ponies were bred on the mainland and by the 1950s there was little need for further exports, so the breed went into decline. However, good management of the ponies has ensured that they have not become extinct in their Shetland home. Today, several hundred of them survive there.

▲ This Shetland foal is just ten days old and will follow its mother closely, learning from her that seaweed is good to eat.

◄ Shetland ponies can be any colour, but are usually dark. Today, owners make little use of the wild ponies, but they remain an integral part of the islanders' lives.

Running wild

Most Exmoor ponies are born in spring, which gives the foals plenty of time to grow and get fit for the winter. This is a time of sunshine and green grass, and the foals spend long periods playing. They caper wildly through the herd on their spindly legs, galloping as fast as they can.

◄ Exmoor foals are born usually between March and September, with most births occurring in April and May. This mare and foal display the true characteristics of the breed, being dark brown in colour with oatmeal-coloured muzzles.

As foals grow older, they will increasingly stray from their mothers' sides, seeking playmates among the other foals in the herd, but at first they stay close.

The Connemara may be black, bay, brown, dun or palomino, but grey is the most usual colour. The only indigenous breed in Ireland, these hardy ponies survive on a diet consisting mainly of rough grass.

Unlike cows, ponies are not ruminants – that is, they do not have a multi-chambered stomach that allows them to digest food several times, with the aid of micro-organisms, regurgitating it for further chewing each time. Like all horses, ponies have a much simpler digestive system with a voluminous intestine that contains a large chamber, called a caecum, stocked with the micro-organisms that assist digestion.

With incisor teeth in both upper and lower jaws, ponies are able to graze the turf short and tight, almost like a lawnmower. The turf is often nibbled so close that it contains very few plant species other than grass, because only grass can tolerate this treatment. This is especially true of areas where large herds gather.

In dry summers, when the grass begins to dry out and its nutritional value declines, ponies have to diversify their feeding patterns and seek out other vegetation, often beside streams. They search for the best places to graze, selecting areas where the grass is lushest.

In winter, however, ponies are often forced to find other sources of food. From autumn onwards, moorland and mountain ponies can be seen nibbling heather, moss, leaves and shrubs such as bramble and gorse, while in the New Forest, some animals even resort to eating spiky holly leaves. Ponies like to eat acorns and may spend hours nosing about among fallen leaves under the oaks in search of this energy-rich food.

Instinctively, they tend to avoid leaving their dung on the best grazing land. Often ponies use the same places year after year and the animals all copy each other and deposit their dung well away from good feeding areas. These communal latrines may also serve, to some extent, as territorial markers.

Social groups

Native ponies live in small groups of females and immature animals led by a dominant mature male. Stallions are highly territorial and can be aggressive, especially in the breeding season. On the other hand, several stallions have been known to share the same grazing. The mares have a clear hierarchy based on seniority. The older ones are dominant and often take over as group leaders if there is no stallion present. Subordinates move aside to allow dominant animals to pass or feed, and the highest-ranked ponies often deposit their own dung or urine on top of that produced by other members of the group.

Ponies spend most of their time standing up, sometimes for several days at a stretch – they can even sleep on their feet. In late summer especially, groups of ponies may be seen standing close to each other for long periods, flicking their tails.

Foals often charge around in groups, barging into each other and occasionally even engaging in mock fighting, with nipping and shoving.

Exmoor foals have short, fluffy manes and tails that reach adult length after about two years.

The young horses' slender legs seem almost in danger of snapping as the youngsters bound through the tussocky grass.

◄ Ponies in the wild, such as these Dartmoors, are gregarious and rarely seen alone. The instinct to form close bonds with other ponies is what keeps the herd together and gives it long-term stability.

▲ For most of the year, Exmoor ponies run wild in small herds of up to 12 or so animals. Although they are free to roam over large tracts of moorland, most remain within an area of about 50 hectares (125 acres).

This behaviour seems to be a way of gaining some protection from biting insects. By standing in groups, head to tail, ponies can swish flies away from each other. This is a useful consequence of living in groups, and probably encourages the animals to congregate and be sociable each day.

Confrontation is rare among ponies. Members of the herd frequently nuzzle each other and indulge in mutual grooming, although there may be the occasional dispute between individuals. Aggressive behaviour includes baring the teeth, sometimes even biting, and moving towards another animal with the neck outstretched and ears held flat. If these threats are ignored, the pony may spin around and kick out with both hind feet.

Breeding battles

The breeding season begins when the ponies moult their thick winter coats at about Easter time. Mares can breed when they are two years old, but many do not do so until later. They are receptive throughout the summer, but matings mostly occur early in the season.

The stallions keep a close eye on their harems, constantly circling the mares and preventing them from wandering off. Sometimes, other stallions may attempt to steal mares from the group and this is when very aggressive behaviour takes place. The competing stallions rear up on their hind legs, lash out with their front hooves and attempt to bite each other.

The mares are pregnant for 11 months and most foals are born from March the following year. Births usually take place at night or around dawn and are over very quickly, often within an hour. In another hour the leggy foal is able to stand up. The mares often mate again soon afterwards, and as they are capable of breeding well into the summer, some will conceive late, which results in foals being born in September, or even later, the following year. These young ponies stay with their mothers throughout winter and continue to suckle until spring.

Mares do not normally produce a new baby every year, but may have two foals in three years. However, the numbers of many native pony herds are affected or controlled by their owners and the way in which these people manage their animals. For instance, young ponies may be separated from their mothers and sold earlier than separation would occur naturally. To avoid distressing the animals, owners are not allowed to sell foals younger than four months old unless they are accompanied by their mothers.

DID YOU KNOW?

Wild ponies, including several non-native types such as Polish Konik ponies, are used to help manage wildlife conservation areas that are threatened by scrub encroachment. The ponies are hardy, so need almost no attention, and they eat and trample their way through brambles, gorse and thickets of unwanted birch scrub. This is particularly valuable on clifftop areas, where the ponies re-create and maintain this vital habitat.

Smell plays a vital role in the social world of ponies. It enables stallions to identify mares in heat and to keep track of potential rivals. Meeting for the first time, these Welsh Mountain ponies sniff each other.

Once the hunting ground of kings, the New Forest has been home to wild ponies since the reign of King Canute (or Cnut) from 1016 to 1035. Foals are born in May and June and are fiercely protected by their mothers.

Hardy survivors

Left to themselves, some native ponies live for more than 20 years, but most die younger than this. Moorlands can be harsh places. In winter, bitingly cold winds and torrential rain are normal. Ponies that live in such environs must endure the weather, day and night. All they can do to protect themselves is seek the meagre shelter provided by deep valleys or clumps of trees and bushes.

A pony's main protection lies in its very thick winter coat. From August onwards, masses of additional fine hairs grow among the hair of the pony's summer coat. This creates an extremely dense mass about 4cm (1½in) deep and gives the animal the appearance of having much thicker legs and a fatter body. The longer hairs that overlie the woolly insulating layer help to direct rainwater away so that it runs down the hairs and drips off without wetting the pony's skin. Long hairs also channel water away from the face and areas of the body vulnerable to chilling when wet. The winter coat is so effective in insulating a pony's body that snow can rest on its back without being melted by body heat.

Superbly adapted to their outdoor existence, native ponies survive the winter on minimum rations until they shed their thick coat the following spring to roam their plentiful summer grazing grounds.

Every autumn, local people in the New Forest hold a series of round-ups or 'drifts'. The wild ponies are herded into enclosures where they receive veterinary attention, are branded and their tails are clipped.

WILDLIFE WATCH

Where can I see native ponies?

● The open moorland of Exmoor, home to the Exmoor ponies, spans the border between Somerset and north Devon. A small herd has also been introduced to the Cumbrian hills.

● Welsh Mountain ponies run wild on some Welsh hills and also in English border county areas, such as the Long Mynd in Shropshire.

● Several herds of Dartmoor ponies live on different parts of Dartmoor. They can be seen from the road from Ashburton to Tavistock and often gather near car parks.

● Shetland ponies are found in small herds on most of the Shetland islands. Those on Unst are the easiest to observe.

● New Forest ponies range freely through the woodland and villages in the New Forest, Hampshire.

● Dales and Fell ponies roam along the eastern and western sides of the Pennines respectively.

● Connemara ponies can be found in Connemara, County Galway, in the west of Ireland.

The pine marten

A nocturnal creature, the agile pine marten bounds through northern forests in a solitary hunt for food, equally at home on the ground or in the trees. This shy creature remains a rare sight despite an increase in its numbers.

The pine marten is one of the native mammals of Britain. Bones found at archaeological sites confirm that it has been present for at least 10,000 years. As recently as 200 years ago it was still widespread throughout mainland Britain, from northern Scotland to the south coast. It lived in the Isle of Wight and even on the fringes of London.

The animal's fine fur and the ease with which it could be snared made it attractive to trappers, and zealous gamekeeping in the 19th century was another devastating blow. As a result, pine marten numbers rapidly dwindled. The species had already become extinct in some English counties by about 1800, and by the 1920s pine martens remained relatively numerous only in north-west Scotland, where there were few people to trouble them.

However, from the 1930s pine marten numbers and distribution showed a steady increase, at least in Scotland. By the mid-1980s, they had returned to Tayside and the Strathclyde region. Natural barriers and heavily built-up areas have made further expansion difficult but not impossible and today there are probably around 3500 pine martens in Scotland.

Meanwhile, a few pine martens were still to be found further south. Even now there are persistent reports of martens being seen, or found dead, in northern England, mainly in the Lake District, Northumberland and north Yorkshire.

Each pine marten has a creamy bib under its chin, which varies in size, tint and shape. This enables individuals to be identified in the wild.

HOME RANGE

The pine marten seems to prefer regions that combine large expanses of mature woodland with patches of open grass. This ensures plenty of logs, undergrowth and bushes for cover and shelter in harsh weather. Grassy glades are also favoured by the voles that are the marten's main prey.

Pine martens are particularly associated with conifer forests but, to some extent, this is forced upon them because conifer plantations are so extensive, especially in Scotland, offering large areas where the animals are relatively safe from gamekeepers. However, pine martens will also live on open moorland and hillsides and even in coastal areas.

Historically, English populations of martens were not restricted to conifer forests and were probably found in a wide variety of habitats.

PINE MARTEN FACT FILE

A cat-sized animal, the pine marten is a relative of the otter, mink and polecat. Very rare over most of Britain, its numbers are slowly increasing, especially in central and western Scotland.

● NAMES
Common name: pine marten
Scientific name: *Martes martes*

● HABITAT
Woodland with patches of open ground and grassy rides

● DISTRIBUTION
Mainly in Scotland, with a few scattered individuals in parts of Wales and northern England; more widespread in Ireland

● STATUS
Rare, but increasing, at least in Scotland

● SIZE
Length (head and body) 50–55cm (20–22in), tail 20–25cm (8–10in); weight (adult male) up to 1.7kg (3lb 12oz). Females about 10% smaller

● KEY FEATURES
Dark brown fur, thick bushy tail, creamy throat patch; short legs; sharp, semi-retractable claws; prominent, triangular ears about 4cm (1½in) long, with pale edges

● HABITS
Mainly active at night and at dusk and dawn, but also active during daylight in summer; solitary

● VOICE
Normally silent, but may growl, hiss and scream when angry; shrill yowl like a cat during mating season

● FOOD
Small mammals, especially voles; fruits, worms, insects, birds' eggs, fish, fruit, fungi, carrion and scraps

● BREEDING
Mates July–August; young (kits) born March–April due to delayed implantation; one litter each year; 1–5 kits (average 3)

● NEST
Makes dens in tree holes, rock crevices and under logs; also uses nestboxes and old squirrel nests

● YOUNG
Similar to adult, but with shorter fur

● SIGNS
Footprints like those of a small dog, usually paired prints; droppings long and black, usually deposited singly in conspicuous locations

The pine marten is a fully protected species. Partly protected by the Wildlife and Countryside Act of 1981, it was granted full protection in 1988 when the legislation was amended to include any den or other structure used by a pine marten for shelter or refuge.

Distribution map key

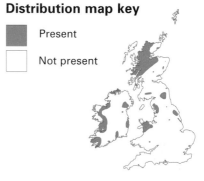

Present

Not present

The ears are particularly prominent and can be rotated to focus on tiny sounds that might betray the presence of prey.

The colour of a pine marten's coat varies considerably during the annual cycle of moults, and also between individuals.

With a long narrow muzzle, the marten has a keen sense of smell.

The long claws are semi-retractable, enabling the marten to run very fast while keeping its claws sharp enough for scrambling up trees, however smooth the bark.

ARBOREAL ABILITY

The pine marten is a member of the weasel family. Uniquely among its relatives, it has semi-retractable claws. These show up prominently in photographs and leave distinct claw marks when the animal crosses soft mud, damp sand or snow, but they retract far enough to stay very sharp. This not only allows the pine marten to run very fast along the ground, but also to scramble up smooth tree trunks and branches.

However, unlike a squirrel, it cannot rotate its ankles to come down a tree head first, hanging by its back feet. Instead, it has to embrace the tree and let itself down tail first in a series of 'jumps', with the hind claws digging in to

Pine martens can leap up to 4m (13ft) from tree to tree. They have also been known to fall 20m (66ft) to the ground and land on their feet, unhurt.

keep a grip. Despite this, it is a very agile creature that can climb, bound and jump among the branches with athletic ease.

As it works its way through the tree tops, the pine marten often discovers birds' nests and devours the eggs. It may also locate the dreys (nests) of squirrels and occasionally it will eat their young. The marten's agility and speed enables it to chase squirrels through the trees, and it may even catch the odd one now and again, especially

inexperienced juveniles. This has given rise to the myth that squirrels are the main food of pine martens, but in reality, chasing full-grown squirrels through the trees would be dangerous and use far more energy than could be obtained from the few actually caught.

In fact, the marten's main mammal prey consists of voles, particularly the field vole, which it catches in woodland glades and on the grassy edges of forest tracks. A marten may eat its catch on the spot, or take it back to its den.

Aways keeping a look-out for prey, the pine marten is also alert to possible danger, although its main enemy is man.

quickly, it uses a bounding action, its back arched high, very different from a cat or any other animal that might be confused with it, except perhaps an otter, mink or polecat. Another distinctive feature is its ears, which are triangular and prominent, about 4cm (1½in) long and with pale edges that emphasise their shape.

Wandering males

Males have larger home territories than females, bordered by natural boundaries such as streams and hedgerows. These boundary areas are often densely marked with droppings. Martens may travel more than 10km (6 miles) in a night, searching for food. Where food is abundant, the animals can restrict themselves to smaller ranges and this increases the potential population density of the region.

During the breeding season, martens trespass on each other's territories

Underground predator

The pine marten is an active hunter, preying on small mammals, such as mice and voles, but also on larger animals, including young rabbits.

Having found and killed a rabbit in its burrow, the marten hauls it out by the ears, dragging the rabbit's limp, heavy body between its front paws.

They never became completely extinct in Wales either, although evidence of their presence is scarce. Reports by reliable observers indicate that some do still live in parts of Wales and northern England, but the total number must be very low, probably fewer than a hundred. It is by no means certain whether these scattered remnants will die out or increase their numbers sufficiently to form viable, secure breeding populations.

Slender hunter

The pine marten is an elusive, swift-moving creature and most sightings are no more than glimpses. At such times the animal resembles a thin cat, but with much shorter legs and a very dark brown coat. Unlike a cat, however, it has a thick furry tail. This is dark, and not banded as in a wildcat. When a marten moves looking for mates but, despite any consequent aggression, fights are rare. Their razor-sharp teeth can deliver a painful and possibly dangerous nip and they are careful to avoid being bitten during confrontations. They are more likely to express their hostility though growls and hissing noises, often spitting like angry cats. Most of the time they simply avoid each other, aided by the scent marks that, left in prominent places, help them to keep track of their neighbours.

Martens make their dens in a variety of places – tree holes, hollow logs, cavities among boulders – and often have several dens within their home territory. They may use nestboxes intended for owls or ducks, and sometimes choose outbuildings. Normally they are nocturnal, but in the higher latitudes of Scotland summer nights are brief and it may not get dark until nearly midnight, with sunrise barely four hours later. This makes it difficult for them to carry out all their activities in

◀ A keen sense of smell allows pine martens to inspect logs and boulders for the telltale scent marks left behind by other martens to advertise their visit.

▼ Berries and fruit form part of the pine marten's diet, as is proved by the mass of undigested remains found in its droppings, rowan berries in this case. Such vegetation does not require as much energy to find and consume as mammal prey.

darkness, especially females trying to collect food for themselves and their young, so martens may occasionally be seen out in daylight, especially in May and June.

Mixed diet

The pine marten's distinctive droppings betray exactly what it has been eating. The droppings are up to 12cm (4⅜in) long, black and twisted like a rope. Often slimy, they dry out in the sun and stay in one piece if they contain fur or feathers. When the animal has been eating mainly berries, its droppings quickly disintegrate in the rain into heaps of pips and fragments of fruit skin. This shows that the pine marten is not just a carnivorous hunter but also eats raspberries, rowan

berries and even fungi. It is certainly not a ravenous killer, and pine martens probably do relatively little damage to gamebird populations. Their destruction by gamekeepers was more to do with prejudice against all predators other than humans, rather than any real threat they posed to grouse or pheasants. However, martens will take advantage of poorly constructed chicken coops if they can

A dead wood pigeon, shot as a farm pest, makes a welcome meal for a marten. Such carrion can be vital to its survival in winter, when it may store fresh bodies under logs and boulders, and return to them later.

Without easing its grip, the marten slips out of the rabbit's warren and pulls its kill clear.

With one front paw on its prize, the marten surveys the surrounding area to check for any potential challenge for its trophy.

Wary hunters

Despite their agility in the trees, pine martens hunt mainly on the ground. However, this makes them vulnerable and they will quickly retreat up a tree if danger threatens.

When moving slowly on the ground, the marten has a lazy bear-like walk, but it can leap and run very fast should the need arise.

▲ Tree holes are a favourite site for dens, providing shelter from the wind and rain. Hollow trees are often hard to find, so the insatiably curious marten will use large nestboxes intended for hole-dwelling ducks, such as the goldeneye, instead.

squeeze their lithe, slim bodies through gaps in woodwork or around ill-fitting doors. They also take a variety of small mammals from voles to young rabbits, as well as squirrels and young birds, which they catch in the trees. In winter they will eat carrion, scavenging the remains of small animals killed by the cold.

Birth control
Pine martens mate in July or August, and the females give birth in March or April of the following year. This might suggest a pregnancy period of more than seven months, which would be a long time for a relatively small mammal. In fact, the pine marten operates what is called 'delayed implantation', whereby the fertilised egg begins development soon after mating but then stops growing for six or seven

months. The egg then implants into the wall of the womb to complete its development, taking about 30 days.

This unusual system is found in a variety of other mammals, including badgers and grey seals. The adaptation ensures that the young are born at the most advantageous time of the year, and in the case of the pine marten, this is early summer. If it had a normal

▼ For a marten, much of the day is spent sleeping before venturing out to search for food at dusk. The animal may look docile when waking up naturally, but it can be very fierce if disturbed, spitting and snarling like an angry cat.

pregnancy period, it would need to mate during the winter when harsh weather and perhaps deep snow can make survival difficult enough without the added stresses of finding a mate. It is far more convenient and efficient for pine martens to find mates in summer, when they are active over wide areas. Delayed implantation also ensures that the babies are not born when the weather is still bad. They would be likely to starve if born in the winter.

The young are born blind and helpless, with sparse whitish fur and weighing about 30g (1oz). Their eyes open at about six weeks, but it is another month before they venture far from the den. Young pine martens become independent between three and four months old, when they resemble their parents except for having rather spindly tails and thinner coats. Their fur thickens in time for winter.

Slow build-up
Pine martens usually mate for the first time at two or three years old and produce one litter per year, of up to five young. They live at very low densities, with perhaps one animal to every 10 square kilometres (4 square miles), which means that the loss of just one or two to traps, illegal shooting, road accidents or natural mortality can leave a big gap in the population. This is one reason why pine martens disappeared from most of Britain relatively quickly and why their reappearance has been slow, despite complete legal protection in recent years.

An attempt to reintroduce the pine marten to certain parts of the country, effectively leapfrogging the obstacles to its

natural distribution, was made in 1980 when a dozen animals were released in Forestry Commission plantations near Dumfries in south-west Scotland. They survived and their numbers have increased. This population has spread, although not very far. There have also been some successful reintroductions in Ireland.

Future plans

The pine marten is a prime candidate for reintroduction to parts of England too and studies are being made to find out whether this would be feasible and likely to succeed. It would be pointless and even cruel to release pine martens if they were

▶ Older martens often have quite a pale, fluffy looking coat.

▼ Although they are superb tree climbers, pine martens, like this one taking a drink at a lakeside, also spend a good deal of time on the ground, where they can move fast with a bounding gait. They have been known to catch fish and can swim, but rarely do so unless absolutely necessary.

likely to die out again as a result of persecution, trapping or road accidents. Even in the remote regions of the far north, where the pine marten is relatively numerous, its survival rate and lifespan is by no means certain in the wild. If the species is to be reintroduced further south, it is important to select areas where the traffic density is low, and where the animals will be tolerated by local farmers and gamekeepers. If reintroduced animals have to face the dangers of traps, illegal poisons and busy roads, they may not be able to cope.

The habitat must be suitable too – dense forestry plantations may not be ideal but other, apparently more natural, regions may be even less adequate. The challenge is made greater by the fact that, owing to its rarity and its elusive nature, the pine marten's basic ecology has not been studied very thoroughly. It remains a slightly mysterious animal.

TERRITORIAL BEHAVIOUR

Pine martens are scarce, secretive and mainly nocturnal. They also live alone, except when the young are with their mother. As a result, they are hard to see in the wild.

The droppings are often the only clue betraying the animal's presence. They are deposited singly and serve as territorial markers, often being placed quite deliberately in prominent places, such as on top of boulders, logs or large grass tussocks. Martens also mark their territory by smearing prominent objects with scent from glands at the base of the tail, a habit that they develop from the age of about four months.

Territorial marking is very important to a solitary species that lives so widely spaced out. Scent messages are the main means of communicating between individuals, and they also help pine martens to find mates. In addition, scent indicates that a territory is occupied and should not be trespassed upon. In this way the animals divide up the habitat and reduce the problems of competing with each other for limited food supplies.

Sense of smell

The pine marten gets its bearings by laying a scent trail. To find this again it must use its nose to identify where it is, even in broad daylight. The sweet musky scent left by the marten makes it fairly easy to track.

WILDLIFE WATCH

Where can I see pine martens?

● Central and western Scotland are the most likely areas to see pine martens.

● You may see one in car headlights as it sprints across the road.

● At some picnic sites martens have taken to searching for scraps and raiding the waste bins.

● Pine martens may feed at garden bird tables in some areas.

● Ask local people if they know where to look.

The kestrel

Patient searching and spectacular dives to earth distinguish this superbly skilled predator. A member of the falcon family, the kestrel patrols open country, keenly alert to any movement on the ground below.

Kestrels are found almost everywhere in the British Isles, in a wide range of habitats, especially rough grassland, much of which is on moorland. Their habit of hanging in the air for long periods, using their powerful eyesight to search the ground for potential prey, makes them easy to spot.

Perceived as beneficial to agriculture because of the large numbers of rodents they destroy, kestrels have suffered less human persecution than other hunting birds, and the species was once Britain's most numerous bird of prey. However, numbers have declined in recent years – perhaps by as much as a third in some places – and now the kestrel is less common in the west of England and in the western Highlands and islands of Scotland.

The prevalence of voles, their principal prey, has a direct effect on kestrels and the reduction in numbers may be a result of intensification of farming. The loss of wide field margins and the increased use of insecticides especially have probably contributed to a decline in the population of voles and other small mammal prey.

Favourite haunts

The kestrel needs reasonably open country, with a combination of short vegetation and trees for perching and nesting. The birds may be seen on mountain, moorland and grassland, on pasture and woodland margins, on heathland, salt marsh, coastal cliffs, over suburban wasteland and sometimes even in large city parks and gardens.

NEST SITES

Kestrels do not construct a nest of their own but seek out a convenient and secure place in which to lay their eggs. They may not breed at all if no suitable site is available. Kestrels usually choose a hollow tree branch, rock ledge or the old nest of another bird, such as a carrion crow or rook. City kestrels often use church towers, or even tall office blocks. Occasionally, kestrels lay their eggs on the ground, in rabbit burrows for instance, but only when there are no alternatives, such as on a small treeless island.

Motorway bridges are a popular choice, free from predators and adjacent to grass verges with a ready supply of voles and other food. However, the young kestrels can be blown out of their niche by passing lorries, or perish in the traffic soon after fledging. To solve this problem, kestrel nestboxes have been installed near some stretches of motorway with great success. For example, on a 14km (8¾ mile) strip of the M40, 11 such boxes were fixed to poles, signs and trees. Made from wood, and waterproofed, the boxes were lined with bark, leaves and wood shavings. The kestrels readily adopted the boxes, and were able to raise their broods in relative safety.

A female kestrel with her week-old chicks. They need plenty of food and grow fast. In years when voles and mice are in short supply, the youngest and weakest members of the brood may die before they fledge.

KESTREL FACT FILE

In flight, the contrast between this medium-sized bird of prey's chestnut body and the pale underside of its wing feathers make it easy to see. Tail feathers splayed into a fan shape give it extra control while it performs its aerial manœuvres. Its habitual 'hovering' is very distinctive.

● NAMES
Common name: kestrel
Scientific name: *Falco tinnunculus*

● HABITAT
Open country

● DISTRIBUTION
Throughout British Isles

● STATUS
Around 50,000 pairs; since around 1990 has declined considerably, especially in the west

● SIZE
Length 32–35cm (12¾–13¾in); wingspan 68–78cm (27½–30¾in); weight 120–300g (4¼–10½oz)

● KEY FEATURES
Slim build, brown plumage with white streaks and black spots; wings long and pointed; dark cheek 'moustache'; yellow feet with black claws; the smaller male has contrasting blue-grey head, rump and tail

● HABITS
Hunts by 'hovering' in the air over open ground for long periods; sometimes hunts from a perch or on the ground

● VOICE
Displaying or agitated birds utter shrill '*kell, kell, kell*' calls; young in nest give loud, thin, drawn-out '*vreee-vreee*' calls when adults visit

● FOOD
Mainly small mammals, especially short-tailed or (field) voles; birds, insects and worms; occasionally reptiles and amphibians

● BREEDING
Early April–early June; one brood per season

● NEST
In a tree hole, or on a cliff or similar ledge, or in old nest of a carrion crow; often nests on buildings in towns and cities, and also on motorway bridges

● EGGS
Usually 4–6 white eggs with reddish brown markings; incubated for 26–34 days, mainly by female

● YOUNG
Downy at first; feathers start to appear at 2 weeks; fledge 27–34 days after hatching; juvenile resembles adult female

Distribution map key

◼ Present

☐ Not present

Both the male and female (shown here) have a yellow eye-ring and 'cere' (bare skin around the external nostrils) that are striking in good light.

Powerful yellow feet with sharp black talons are used for gripping prey, and the long toes give the foot a broad span. When the bird cleans its talons and feet, it uses its sharply hooked bill in a surprisingly delicate fashion.

The long tail has a black band near the end and a white tip. Kestrels often overlap their tail feathers when perched.

Young kestrels pluck up the courage to take their first flight. They will continue to be fed and guarded by their parents for several weeks thereafter.

THE KESTREL CALENDAR

JANUARY • FEBRUARY

Young kestrels from the previous season sometimes stay with their parents for several months. By January and February, however, the courting adults, who usually remain paired throughout the year, will start to resent the presence of last year's youngsters in their territory.

MARCH • APRIL

Breeding pairs of kestrels continue their courtship displays and then select a nest site. The female lays her clutch of eggs, often in mid to late April. She is primarily responsible for incubation, although the male will take short turns at sitting on the eggs.

MAY • JUNE

An almost continual supply of voles and other small mammals is brought back to the nest for the young. Initially, the parents may dismember the prey into small pieces, but as the chicks grow they are increasingly allowed to tackle the problems of feeding themselves.

JULY • AUGUST

The young are almost ready to leave the nest. It is not unusual for as few as two youngsters to fledge from an initial brood of four or five. There is fierce competition for food among the chicks, and the strongest may even kill the weakest.

SEPTEMBER • OCTOBER

The young kestrels have left their parents' territory by this time. Those that hatched late have a higher mortality rate than early hatching broods because they have not been fed for so long. They are also unlikely to find a territory near home.

NOVEMBER • DECEMBER

In harsh winters the resident birds may find it difficult to survive as rodents hide underground and become harder to find. Kestrels may have to switch to alternative prey, including small birds, shrews or even earthworms if the opportunity arises.

Kestrels frequently hunt over the green corridors provided by the verges of major roads. A kestrel hanging in the sky, seemingly immobile, close to a motorway's hard shoulder, is a common sight.

Over much of southern Britain, kestrels are resident throughout the year, but farther north and west many, especially immature birds, migrate south at the end of the breeding season, returning to set up a territory the following spring. In winter, many kestrels arrive in Britain from farther north and east, mainly from the Netherlands and Scandinavia. Food shortages may result in migrations, and those breeding on high moorland often move down to lower ground in winter, when the hills are covered by snow.

Hunting and feeding habits

When hunting, the kestrel seems to 'hover' for prolonged periods, about 10–40m (30–130ft) above the ground. It keeps its head absolutely still in order to detect the slightest movement on the ground below. Every other part of its body moves to compensate for this, while the head appears to be held by an invisible clamp. The splayed tail is constantly

adjusted, rudder-like, to allow for changes in the wind. Every so often the bird will select a fresh position and continue its watch. When a target is accurately sighted, the bird suddenly drops vertically to the ground and grabs the prey in its talons, before dispatching it swiftly with a bite. To save energy while hunting, a kestrel may use a convenient perch, such as a tree, pylon, bridge or even a fencepost, from which to scan the ground for prey.

Although the kestrel eats mainly small rodents, such as mice and voles, it is an adaptable bird and may sometimes

▲ The adult male kestrel is smaller than the female, and distinguished by its blue-grey head, rump and tail, which contrasts with the chestnut-coloured plumage on the rest of its body.

◄ Like other birds of prey, kestrels will often take a 'perch and pounce' approach to catching food, sometimes using quite low lookout points, such as fenceposts.

remain on the ground, searching for insects, earthworms and even snails. It will take smaller birds when it can catch them and the occasional reptile or amphibian. The kestrel is not skilled at catching birds in flight, but may manage to seize nestlings or newly fledged songbirds, such as starlings, house sparrows or finches. Some kestrels are adept at snatching birds from garden bird tables, which means they may sometimes be wrongly identified as sparrowhawks.

Courtship and breeding

Aerial chases, sometimes in circles high in the sky, are a ritual of courtship. The male may dive repeatedly towards a sitting female, who ducks as he approaches, and he may fly with rapid wingbeats interspersed with long glides. Kestrels remain paired for the season, sometimes for life. The male catches and presents food to the female as part of the pair-bonding process.

A clutch of four to six eggs is laid between early April and early June, the timing varying from year to year. The eggs are whitish, with heavy reddish brown markings. The female is the main incubator, and the young hatch after 26 to 34 days, the smaller male chicks hatching a couple of days before the females.

On hatching, the chicks are sparsely covered with fine white down, which darkens and thickens over the following week. At about two weeks old, the first contour feathers begin to appear through the down, and by about day 24 the flight and tail feathers have emerged. By 34 days old the young bird is fully fledged and will start to exercise its wings and practise flapping movements.

During the period that the young birds stay in the nest, first the male and then both parents bring them food. After a further 30 days or so, the young become independent and catch prey for themselves, usually moving away from their home territories at this stage.

Hunting technique

The seemingly effortless way in which a kestrel is able to hang in the air, appearing to be stationary, is one of the marvels of nature The moment prey is located, the bird plunges earthwards.

The kestrel hunts over open country, where its apparent hover is, in fact, a slow flight into the wind. All of the bird is in motion apart from its head, which is fixed in relation to the ground.

Having made a successful hunt, this female kestrel brings a short-tailed vole back to feed her young, hidden in a tree hole.

Before going in for the kill, the bird may pull in its wings slightly in order to lose height, and then 'hover' again nearer the ground. This allows it to scrutinise its prey more closely.

The bird will often drop to the ground gradually, using the spread and angle of its wings and tail to execute fine control over its descent.

If speed is of the essence, the bird may use strong, direct flight to accelerate its descent towards the ground, thus reducing the chance of its quarry escaping.

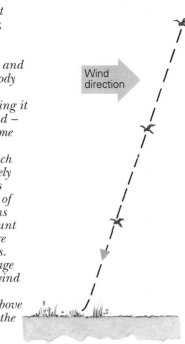

USING THE WIND

The kestrel does not truly hover. Rather, it makes minute adjustments to the angles of its wings and tail to control its body in headwinds and updraughts, enabling it to hang in the wind – an old country name for the kestrel is 'windhover'. At such times, its head barely moves. This skill is central to its mode of hunting and means that kestrels can hunt in open areas where there are no perches. An added advantage of flying into the wind is that the final approach is both above and downwind of the intended prey.

Wind direction

The cuckoo

The familiar call of this visitor is a welcome signal of approaching summer. Famously, the cuckoo relies on a variety of other birds to raise its young, which are usually considerably larger than the foster parents.

The lifecycle of the cuckoo has been widely documented, from the distinctive call of the male to the species' unusual breeding habits. Although it is present in a wide range of habitats throughout most of the British Isles and is frequently heard, it is not an easy bird to spot.

The cuckoo's range is determined mainly by the distribution of the host species, the nests of which it parasitises, but also by the availability of its favourite food – insects. It shows a particular preference for caterpillars, especially hairy caterpillars or those with warning colours, which are unpalatable or even poisonous to many other birds. In addition, female cuckoos often consume the eggs of the host bird.

Spring arrivals

Cuckoos begin to arrive in early April, and the males begin to make their familiar '*cu-coo*' calls soon after, with the emphasis on the first syllable. Sometimes a male gives a three-syllable variant, such as '*cu-cu-coo*' or '*cu-coo-coo*', especially if it is excited. However, not all cuckoo calls are what they seem – the collared dove occasionally leaves out a syllable of its trisyllabic '*cu-COO-coo*' call, so can sound quite cuckoo-like at a distance.

The female cuckoos answer the males' advertising calls with a somewhat drawn-out bubbling trill, which in fact is just as easy to recognise, but less well-known. Before long, the cuckoos pair up ready for mating. They use stealth to find the nests of host birds. At this stage, smaller birds may mob cuckoos, rather as they would a roosting owl, despite the fact that the cuckoo resembles a feared predator of adult songbirds, the sparrowhawk. Research suggests that songbirds are well able to distinguish between cuckoos and birds of prey, and may be aware that cuckoos pose a threat to their eggs but not to themselves.

After her eggs have formed and are ready to be laid, the female cuckoo watches carefully from a tree or other suitable perch. She is a patient and careful observer of her host's behaviour.

The gaping orange-red mouth of this young cuckoo is enough to awaken the feeding instinct in its meadow pipit foster parent, despite the dramatic disparity in size between the adult bird and the fledgling.

CUCKOO FACT FILE

Cuckoos resemble a cross between a kestrel and a sparrowhawk, but cuckoos neither hang in the wind nor soar, flying direct with low wingbeats in which the wings beat rapidly and deeply. Cuckoos frequently glide, especially before landing.

● NAMES
Common name: cuckoo
Scientific name: *Cuculus canorus*

● HABITAT
Depends on the host species they use; includes heathland, bushy moorland, farmland, woodland and also reedbeds, marshes and fens

● DISTRIBUTION
Spring and summer visitor; found all over the British Isles except Orkney and Shetland, where it is scarce or sporadic

● STATUS
Estimated at 13,000–26,000 pairs in Britain with another 3000–6000 pairs in Ireland

● SIZE
Length 32–34cm (12¾–13½in); weight about 120g (4¼oz)

● KEY FEATURES
Cuckoos are slender and dove-sized, with a long tail and narrow pointed wings; the spring and summer call of the male is distinctive

● HABITS
Secretive; during the spring and summer spends more time perched than flying. The newly hatched birds heave all the host's eggs (and sometimes nestlings) out of the nest

● VOICE
Far-carrying *'cu-coo'* from male; female's typical bubbling call heard in breeding season; both sexes utter harsh *'gowk gowk gowk'* call, especially in flight or when alighting on a perch

● FOOD
Primarily insects and their larvae; fond of hairy caterpillars and those with warning coloration that are unpleasant or toxic to other birds

● BREEDING
Eggs laid in May and June

● NEST
Female lays her eggs in the nests of various other birds, which then raise the young cuckoo instead of their own brood

● EGGS
Very variable, depending on the host species used; a female may lay up to 25 eggs in a season; incubation takes 11–13 days

● YOUNG
Usually larger than host species; fledge 17–21 days after hatching

The eyes, base of the bill and the feet are yellow.

The adult cuckoo has uniformly pale to slate grey upperparts.

Below the grey throat and upper breast, the underparts are marked with thin black bars. Females are slightly browner than males, especially on the breast where the barring begins.

A perched cuckoo typically adopts a horizontal or semi-horizontal posture, with wings held drooping below the line of the body.

Distribution map key

Present during summer months

BROOD PARASITE

One theory for the cuckoo's parasitic behaviour explains the advantages it gives to the species. Adult cuckoos eat noxious insects that many other birds find distasteful, or even poisonous. These might not be the best food for young cuckoos, or at least not as nutritious as the food offered by other species. This means that nestlings reared elsewhere might be at an advantage over those reared by the cuckoos themselves. The young cuckoo's instinctive clearing of the nest of other eggs or newly hatched chicks maximises its food supply.

During the breeding season, the female cuckoo may spend many hours watching, waiting for the right moment. Once a nest has been located, she moves in quickly and with great secrecy to deposit a single egg into the nest, while the host bird is still in the process of completing her own clutch, but before incubation has started.

If a host notices a cuckoo at or near its nest, it will attack it and try to drive it away, and will also then be more likely to desert its own clutch. It therefore pays the cuckoo to minimise time spent in the host's nest – she can lay her egg in just a few seconds and be away again before the host has even detected her presence.

Selecting a host

Egg laying begins in May, with each female laying up to 25 times in a season. Sometimes the cuckoo removes one or two eggs from the host's nest, so that the overall total remains roughly the same. She will lay one egg every other day, usually during the afternoon, and for each egg she selects a different host nest, although usually of the same host species. The number of host birds adopted by

◄ Cuckoos are not often photographed flying, as they tend to take off suddenly and quickly seek cover. Their flight is usually low and quite fast, with the wings never rising above the birds' backs.

▲ In the breeding season, cuckoos spend more of their time perched on a suitable vantage point than flying. Males are looking for females, while females watch out for host nests in which to lay their eggs.

cuckoos runs to over 100 species, but individual cuckoos apparently specialise in one species. Even in Britain, more than 50 species are known to have been chosen, although four hosts account for more than 80 per cent of all records.

The commonest British host species are the meadow pipit (on moorland in Ireland and the uplands of north and west Britain), dunnock (in woodland and farmland in south and central England), reed warbler (in marshland, especially

in East Anglia) and pied wagtail (on moorland and in open farmland and pasture). Other moorland hosts include the whinchat and skylark.

There are probably four genetically distinct races of cuckoo in Britain, each specialising in a different main host species and each laying a particular type of egg, usually – but not always – matching those of their host. Thus 'wagtail-cuckoos' lay pale, greyish eggs, 'reed warbler-cuckoos' lay greenish eggs and 'meadow pipit-cuckoos' lay brownish eggs.

Some host birds seem able to discriminate between their own eggs and those of the cuckoo, unless the match is very close. This is why, over time, cuckoo eggs have evolved so that they are difficult to tell from those of their hosts. In parts of Europe, they match perfectly with host eggs as varied as those of the redstart (pure blue), robin (pale with reddish spots) and great reed warbler (greenish-white with dark blotches). On the other hand, in Britain 'dunnock-cuckoo' eggs are pale and spotted, clashing with the pure pale blue of those of their host, but dunnocks seem unable to distinguish between their own and cuckoo eggs.

One study of 'reed warbler-cuckoos' showed that the females remove the eggs and chicks from nests that they are not yet ready to use. This forces the warblers to lay a second clutch, which the cuckoos can then take over.

CUCKOO CALENDAR

OCTOBER ● FEBRUARY

Cuckoos overwinter in Africa, probably mainly south of the equator. Their arrival in Africa coincides with the start of the rainy season in the equatorial region and beyond, which means that there are abundant supplies of insect food in the savanna (above) and humid forests.

MARCH ● MAY

In March the cuckoos begin flying north again. When they arrive in April, the male birds announce their presence with their characteristic calls. Also sometimes heard is the strange bubbling call of the female, answering the male during courtship. The female begins to lay eggs in May.

JUNE ● JULY

The young cuckoos hatch and grow fast, rapidly becoming larger than their foster parents. Without responsibility for raising their chicks, adult cuckoos begin to leave towards the end of July, making the species one of the earliest of summer visitors to leave the British Isles.

AUGUST ● SEPTEMBER

Adult migration southwards is now well under way, to the wintering grounds south of the Sahara. Juveniles (above) begin to fend for themselves at this time, leaving the foster nest and building strength for their long first trip south about a month after their parents.

Nest invader

A female cuckoo selects several nests of the host species in which to lay her eggs. When the cuckoo's egg hatches, the young cuckoo ensures that it will be the only chick in the nest by pushing out all the other eggs. In this way, the impostor monopolises all the food brought by its foster parents and soon grows to a size quite disproportionate to the host's nest. The foster parents continue to feed the young cuckoo even though it bears little resemblance to a nestling of their own species.

In a meadow pipit's nest, a cuckoo's egg has been added to the clutch. The cuckoo's egg hatches first because the time it needs for incubation is slightly shorter than that needed by a meadow pipit egg.

Few sights are as bizarre as two small adult songbirds hurrying to feed their enormous 'adopted' chick. Once fledged, cuckoos are so demanding that they may successfully solicit feeding by other birds, as well as by their foster parents.

After about a month, the young cuckoo becomes more independent, seeking food for itself. It leaves the hatching area and starts eating insects and their larvae, building up strength and vital reserves for its first migration.

Heading south

Adult cuckoos begin to leave Britain in mid July, while their young are still being cared for by their foster parents. The juveniles make their migration a little later, in August or September, never having seen their actual parents. This means that they cannot learn their migration route from their parents, so navigation must be instinctive. The precise wintering grounds of cuckoos have not been mapped, but most of them probably cross the Mediterranean and the Sahara to equatorial or even southern Africa.

Eight to ten hours after hatching, the nestling cuckoo follows its instinctive urge to destroy all the other eggs in the nest. One by one, it manoeuvres the eggs to lie in the sensitive hollow of its back. Head held down, wings spread out and feet splayed, it heaves each egg up to the rim of the nest until finally the egg topples over the edge. At the end of this operation, the young cuckoo has the whole nest to itself.

WILDLIFE WATCH

Where can I see cuckoos?

● From April to August, cuckoos can be found in a range of habitats, including open moors, heathland, grassland, woodland, scrub, farmland, marshes and reedbeds.

● Cuckoos tend to prefer areas that combine cover with occasional taller vantage points, such as rocks or trees.

● As a rule, cuckoos avoid dense forest, very bare or exposed regions and built-up areas.

● Although the cuckoo is a relatively common species, good sightings are often a matter of luck.

The young bird's bright, orange-red gape is enough to elicit the instinctive feeding response of its hosts. Unlike other nestlings, which close their bills quickly over the food, the young cuckoo leaves its mouth gaping wide open until the smaller foster parent is safely out of the way – otherwise it risks injuring its provider. By the time it is about two weeks old, the young cuckoo weighs more than three and a half times its foster parent's weight.

The hobby

A slim and elegant falcon, the hobby is a summer visitor to the British Isles.
One of the most aerobatic birds of prey, it performs dazzling display flights, and its
skills in the air also allow it to catch fast-moving dragonflies and small birds.

**Seen head on, the hobby reveals
distinctive facial markings. The long,
narrow wings are typical of all
falcons. The spread tail aids
manoeuvrability on the wing.**

The hobby is one of the world's most agile and graceful birds of prey. It is also among the fastest, with an impressive turn of speed that equips it for capturing some of the swiftest and most elusive aerial prey. A strikingly handsome species, the hobby is Britain's only breeding bird of prey that feeds mainly on insects, particularly dragonflies. During the breeding season, however, it switches its diet to a variety of mostly small birds. It also hunts bats at dusk. The sight of one of these quicksilver falcons in pursuit of its quarry can be breathtaking.

The hobby is a long-distance traveller. Its streamlined body and long, narrow wings enable it to undertake an annual migration of 4000km (2500 miles) or more from wintering grounds in Africa, south of the Sahara, to breeding grounds in Britain. The first birds arrive in

mid-April but latecomers may not turn up until mid-May. Like many other migratory birds of prey, hobbies usually circle upwards on thermals (rising pockets of warm air) to gain height and thus reduce energy expenditure when migrating over land. However, crossing the sea requires considerable effort because thermals do not form over water. To prepare for the final flight over the English Channel, the birds often stop to feed in northern France before setting out.

Spring gathering

When they first arrive, hobbies gather in small numbers at traditional feeding areas on the south coast to rest and replenish their energy stores before moving on to their breeding territories. Heaths with good populations of large moths, ponds and bogs with plenty of dragonflies, and

lakes or river valleys with abundant aquatic insects are the most popular sites, and many are visited year after year.

The hobby is a skilled hunter, plucking darting dragonflies from the air with seemingly effortless precision. From high, gliding flight, a powerful beat of the bird's wings produces a burst of speed that enables it to close in rapidly on a flying insect. With a swift flick of its wings and tail, the hobby jinks sideways, swinging its talons forward to secure another morsel.

Insects are usually consumed in flight, the hobby bringing its feet forward to its bill in a single, smooth movement. The hard parts of the insect, such as its legs and wing cases, are neatly severed and discarded, drifting to the ground, while the hobby begins the search for other airborne prey.

HOBBY FACT FILE

One of the smaller birds of prey, the hobby is a long-winged falcon. In flight, it appears swift-like, with scythe-shaped wings and a shortish tail. In summer it may be seen soaring and flying over moors and heaths in search of small bird and insect prey.

● **NAMES**
Common names: hobby, northern hobby
Scientific name: *Falco subbuteo*

● **HABITAT**
Open heaths, downs, farmland and woodland edges with feeding areas and trees for nesting; before and after migration often gathers at lakes, reedbeds and bogs

● **DISTRIBUTION**
Mainly in south and east but increasingly further north as far as southern Scotland

● **STATUS**
Summer visitor; increasing from fewer than 200 pairs in early 1950s to perhaps as many as 1000 pairs in 2004

● **SIZE**
Length 30–36cm (11¾–14¼in); weight 130–330g (4⅝–11⅝oz), female heavier than male

● **KEY FEATURES**
Slate grey above; pale grey unbarred tail and white half-collar on nape; heavily streaked underparts with rusty red 'trousers' and undertail coverts; dark cap, white chin

● **HABITS**
Solitary hunter; swift and agile in flight

● **VOICE**
Silent outside breeding season, but vocal during courtship and near nest; main call a shrill '*kew-kew-kew*'

● **FOOD**
Moths, beetles, dragonflies, damselflies and other insects; also house and sand martins, swallows and other birds, including swifts and larks; occasionally bats

● **BREEDING**
Return to former territories from mid-May; eggs laid in June; single brood

● **NEST**
Adopts old nests of crows and other large birds

● **EGGS**
2–4 brown-yellow eggs speckled with reddish-brown; incubated mainly by female for 28–32 days

● **YOUNG**
Fledge at 28–34 days; fed by both parents in nest and for another 21–35 days after fledging; juvenile resembles adult but browner with buff underparts

The eye ring and the bare skin at the base of the bill are yellow.

Dark and white facial markings produce a 'mask' effect.

The back and upper side of the wings are a dark slate grey. In adults with worn plumage, like this one, they have a brownish tinge.

Legs and feet are yellow.

The long, narrow wings have blackish tips.

From the front, a hobby is a well-marked bird with bold dark streaks on a creamy white breast.

Distribution map key

Present during summer months

Not present

The hobby is fully protected at all times by the Wildlife and Countryside Act 1981. Under Schedule 1, it is an offence to kill hobbies or disturb their nests and young.

Aerial skills

The hobby is an unusual bird of prey because for much of the year its diet comprises mainly insects, particularly large species of dragonfly and beetle. Catching fast-flying insects in flight is no mean feat and the bird needs to use all of its prowess in the air to guarantee a successful hunt.

As the bird plucks the beetle from the air, it brings its wings forward to counteract the shift in weight and drag caused by extending the legs.

A lithe and graceful flier, the hobby's wingbeats seem relaxed and effortless.

When the hobby spots a large beetle in flight, it prepares to snatch the insect, swivelling its tail to adjust its direction.

Bringing its feet forward to either side of its bill, with talons outspread, the hobby gets ready to strike.

HOBBY CALENDAR

APRIL • JUNE

Hobbies arrive in Britain from mid-April. Pairs meet up from mid-May and perform spectacular display flights over their territories before taking over disused nests. The first birds lay their eggs in June.

JULY

One month later, the downy chicks hatch. They are brooded by the female while the male provides food, mainly small birds. The young grow quickly on up to nine meals a day.

AUGUST • SEPTEMBER

The juveniles fledge in August, but remain dependent on their parents for food while they practise the hunting skills they will need to survive. Soon the adults will leave their offspring and head south.

OCTOBER • MARCH

By mid-October, all the hobbies have left Britain to start their long migration to the tropics for the winter, where their moult is completed. In March, the first birds begin the return journey northwards.

Later in the season, hobbies change from feeding mainly on insects to taking a wide range of small birds that habitually fly in the open, away from cover. Common prey includes larks, pipits, wagtails, sparrows, starlings, martins, swallows and even swifts. Hobbies breed later than many other birds of prey, probably in order to take advantage of the large numbers of unwary juvenile songbirds that fledge from July onwards. They also rob other birds – especially kestrels – of their bird or mammal prey.

Hobbies prefer to eat insects on the wing, occasionally landing if their prey proves to be too energetic to subdue in flight. However, birds would usually be consumed on a perch or on the ground.

...then eats its prey a little at a time, slowing down slightly as it concentrates on feeding.

Airspeed is regained in a shallow dive. The broadly spread wings are characteristic of an insect-hunting hobby.

Spreading its tail for balance, the hobby passes the prey to its bill, still grasping it in its talons.

The hobby removes the beetle's hard, inedible wing cases and legs, and drops them...

From mid-May onwards, hobbies return to their traditional breeding territories, which may be used for up to four years in succession. Although breeding pairs sometimes travel together, the male is usually first to arrive. He soon begins a spectacular display flight to advertise his presence, racing over the treetops in a zig-zagging dash. When the female returns, the pair continue to display, performing exceptionally fast chases. They soar high in the sky, the male diving at the female and often looping the loop, while she flips on to her back.

A pair of hobbies generally return to a favourite nest site to breed, but many birds also have alternative eyries, or nests, that they use in turn. These falcons never build their own nests. The late timing of their breeding season means that they are able to adopt empty crow's nests, the young occupants of which may have fledged a few days earlier. Nest sites usually have a commanding view over the surrounding countryside. The first eggs are laid in June, the female undertaking most of the incubation, while the male provides food.

Defending the nest

In the month that follows, the hobbies stay on or near the nest, except when marauding crows or magpies venture too close. Then the off-duty bird will swoop at the intruder in an attempt to force it away. These attacks are usually successful,

▲ Throughout the breeding season, and especially when feeding young, the hobby is an excellent bird catcher. Larks, starlings, blackbirds, swallows and swifts are at risk from May to August.

◄ As with most other bird eaters, hobbies pluck their prey before consuming it. This feeding technique is especially important when the meal is being offered to young chicks in the nest.

▶ Initially, the chicks are fed by the female. She tears up the prey into pieces small enough for the nestlings to digest and feeds each chick in turn.

▼ At 21 days old, this hobby chick is beginning to lose its white down and acquire the brown upperpart plumage and facial markings of a juvenile. It will fledge within a week or so, but remain dependent on its parents for a further three to five weeks.

but some hobby nests are robbed by crows. If this happens early in the season, the pair may lay another clutch.

For the first 10 days, the white, downy young are brooded exclusively by the female, but later she will watch over them from a nearby branch or a neighbouring tree. Meanwhile, the male catches birds to feed the brood, presenting the specially plucked prey to the female, who feeds

bite-sized morsels to each chick in turn. Once the young are old enough to be alone for a short time, the female leaves the nest to meet the male on his return from a hunting trip. As he approaches the nest, the male calls to his mate and she flies up to greet him. The male glides slowly, while the female flips briefly on to her side or back to take the prey directly from his talons. Alternatively, he may drop the food for her to catch in mid-air.

When the chicks are about two weeks old, they do not wait to be fed, but start to tear at the prey in the female's talons.

There is very little sibling rivalry early on and, unlike those of some birds of prey, hobby chicks rarely attack each other. However, as they approach fledging, the youngsters become more aggressive and begin to squabble over food. The female leaves them to fight it out among themselves. The first chick to grab the meal usually carries it to the edge of the nest and covers it with its outspread wings, a form of behaviour known as mantling. Survival becomes a constant battle in which only the strongest and fittest young are likely to succeed.

On heaths and farmland, the hobby may be seen perching on fences and gates as well as tree branches. Even from these low vantage points, it can still scan the surrounding countryside for prey.

◄ Hobbies make attentive parents and one adult is nearly always in attendance at the nest. During the height of summer, the parents shelter their chicks from the heat of the sun by spreading their wings over them.

▼ When perched in trees, a hobby can be difficult to spot, but when it arrives on its nesting territory in spring it will sometimes perch conspicuously.

Even after they have fledged, the young continue to beg food from their parents. The adults give special food calls as they fly past and by watching the female take prey from the male in mid-air, the young learn the necessary techniques to perform aerial food passes. They are slow and clumsy at first, but soon improve. Occasionally, the juveniles may try to beg food from other pairs of hobbies, or even from kestrels.

Learning to hunt

Within one or two weeks, the young hobbies learn to hunt insects for themselves, honing their technique through long aerial games with their siblings. They may even attempt to catch birds and bats under the guidance of their parents. Despite the juveniles' increasing proficiency at hunting, the adults continue to supplement their diet for up to five weeks after they fledge.

By early September, the young are able to fend for themselves and their parents can leave them. The juveniles remain together as a family group and begin to wander widely – usually southwards – in search of a good place to feed. At this time of year, it is possible to see a dozen or more young hobbies together on the south coast. Most birds will have dispersed by the end of September to begin the long journey south. Migrating hobbies are usually observed as single birds or in small groups of two to five individuals.

Increasing population

The hobby is one of Britain's scarcest birds of prey. In the late 1960s, it was estimated that there were about 100 breeding pairs, down from 200 in the early 1950s. However, despite the pressures of egg collecting and the popular southern European pastime of shooting migrating birds of prey, hobby numbers have been increasing in Britain. Today, its population is believed to exceed the 1960s total by at least five times and possibly as much as ten times.

One factor in the hobby's recovery is that it was one of the few birds of prey to escape the effects of the use of pesticides in the late 1950s and 1960s. Pesticides built up in the bodies of animals that fed on dressed seed, such as rodents and pigeons, in turn harming the birds that hunted them. The hobby's diet of aerial insects and small birds meant it was largely unaffected.

In recent years, hobbies have expanded northwards and are now to be found not just on southern heathlands and downlands, but in a much greater variety of open places with scattered trees.

WILDLIFE WATCH

Where can I see hobbies?

● Heathland and moors in Dorset, Surrey, Sussex and the New Forest, and southern downland, such as the South Downs, are good places to find hobbies. They visit wetlands and reedbeds to hunt and are also colonising lowland habitats.

● Hobbies breed in good numbers south of a line between the Mersey and Humber estuaries and across the English-Welsh border. Small but increasing numbers breed to the north and west.

● A few weeks after the birds arrive in Britain in mid-April, they move from the south coast to breeding territories on moors and heaths, where they start performing their exciting aerial displays.

These are breathtaking to watch but great care should be taken not to disturb the birds at this stage of their breeding cycle. They are very sensitive to disturbance and may even abandon any breeding attempts for the year.

● The hobby is a protected species and should never be disturbed in its nesting territories. If a bird flies around a group of people uttering high-pitched calls, they are too close and should move away.

● The best time to watch for hobbies is between mid-August and late September, after the young have fledged and before the birds begin their long migration south.

The adder

Superbly camouflaged to blend in with almost any background, this timid snake will slide into the undergrowth at the first hint of danger. Approach with care to see one basking on a wall, rock or mat of bracken in the sun.

When a basking adder is disturbed, it adopts an aggressive posture. Its eyes focus directly towards the perceived threat, its neck curls back ready to strike, and it often hisses menacingly.

Found all over the mainland and on some offshore islands (but not in Ireland), the adder has the distinction of being the only venomous snake in Britain. Heaths, dunes and other open land, as well as woodlands and reedbeds, are among its favourite locations. The adder population has declined in recent years due to the planting of moorland with conifer trees, the conversion of rough pasture into arable land and urban development, but this land snake remains fairly common wherever good basking sites are available.

Small appetite

The adder hunts by day for a variety of small mammals, mainly voles and mice, but it also takes lizards, nestling birds, birds' eggs and occasionally frogs. Other more unusual food items include slow-worms, weasels and moles. Young adders appear to feed mainly on baby mammals and small lizards.

Snakes are cold-blooded, which means their body temperature is dictated by their surroundings. Consequently, they have no need to use up energy to keep warm, as warm-blooded mammals and birds must, and so need less food. They can go without eating for long periods, particularly in cooler weather and, of course, while hibernating. Indeed, the feeding season is short and in a whole year an adult adder may eat as little as the equivalent of just nine voles. When they emerge from hibernation in spring, male adders do not feed until they have found a mate, and pregnant females fast until after their young are born in August.

Adders have two hunting strategies. They either lie in ambush in promising spots, their bodies coiled ready to strike, or – if the weather is warm enough – they go looking for prey, investigating animal burrows and even climbing into low shrubs in search of nestling birds.

A hunting adder locates its prey by smell, using its forked tongue to gather scent from the air. It pinpoints its target by sight at the last minute, relying on the creature making some movement to betray its position. The adder then creeps forward, curving the front section of its body into an 'S' shape. When the animal moves again, the adder strikes, shooting its head forward to stab its quarry with its fangs and inject poison. It releases the creature immediately to avoid being caught by snapping teeth or swiping claws.

ADDER FACT FILE

Britain's most widespread reptile, the adder may be found on open heaths and moorland and in upland locations. Distinguished by a dark zigzag pattern on its back and a 'V' shaped mark on the head, the adder may shed its skin several times during its lifetime.

● NAMES
Common names: adder or northern viper
Scientific name: *Vipera berus*

● HABITAT
Wide range of upland, lowland, dry and wet sites with suitable basking areas, including heaths, moors, bogs, dunes, woods, meadows; also basks on shingle ridges, sea-wall defences, railway embankments and quarries

● DISTRIBUTION
Patchy over much of mainland Britain, Isle of Wight, Anglesey, Isle of Man and some of Inner Hebrides; none in Ireland

● STATUS
Less common than in recent past; scarce in many areas

● SIZE
Up to 65cm (2ft 2in) long; male smaller than female; record females have reached almost 90cm (3ft)

The adder is protected against deliberate killing, injury or sale by the Wildlife and Countryside Act, 1981. Sadly, many people still persecute adders illegally.

● KEY FEATURES
Males have black dorsal zigzag on whitish or cream to straw-coloured background, sometimes tinged bluish or greenish; females have sandy or brownish to reddish background; undersides of both sexes greyish, brownish or bluish, with paler, dull yellowish or whitish throat with dark spots; eye has vertical black pupil and reddish iris

● HABITS
Nocturnal; normally solitary, does not defend territory; prey immobilised by venom and swallowed whole

● VOICE
Sharp hiss when irritated or threatened

● FOOD
Small mammals, birds' eggs and nestlings, frogs, toads, newts, lizards, slow-worms; adults favour short-tailed voles

● BREEDING
Mating occurs April–early May. Female produces 3–18 (average 9) live young, usually in late August, every other year; eggs hatch and develop into young within female's body; young may be covered with a thin membrane at birth

● YOUNG
Similar to parents; 14–18cm (5½–7in) at birth; reddish or orangey brown; grow 8–12cm (3–5in) per year until sexually mature at 3–4 years

● SIGNS
Discarded skins where adders are abundant

Adders sometimes bask in groups, preferring gentle warmth to the strong heat of the midday sun.

Distribution map key

■ Present

☐ Not present

Males have a pale, creamy ground colour; females are browner.

The eyes have elliptical pupils that open wide in dim light, enabling the adder to hunt small mammals in the dark of their burrows.

The scales are made of dry keratin embedded in skin and are dry, smooth and polished.

The prey usually succumbs to the adder's venom after two or three minutes, by which time it may have fled some distance away. The adder can easily find it by following its scent and may even pursue small mammals into their burrows where, if there is a litter of young, it includes them in its meal as well.

Venomous bite

The poison is delivered by two fangs 7mm (¼in) long, which hinge forward on either side of the upper jaw when the snake opens its mouth. Each fang is connected to a venom gland behind the eye. If the snake loses a fang, it has others that move forward to take its place.

The venom, a form of saliva, is haemotoxic, which means it destroys red blood cells and causes blood vessels to rupture. As a result, the prey's body

▲ Adders become sluggish and eventually retreat into hibernation when average temperatures drop below 8°C (46°F). Warm winter days may tempt them out despite a dusting of snow on the ground.

▶ The adder locates prey using its sense of smell, flicking its tongue to gather scent particles from the air and transfer them to a special scent receptor, the Jacobson's organ, located in the roof of the mouth.

Dance of the adders

In spring, males seek out females but often other males will intrude in the mating ritual. If interrupted, a courting male will display aggressively to his rival and the two may wrestle to decide who wins the right to mate.

The first male chases the intruder, the pair sometimes moving in parallel as if courting, with the first male blocking his rival's path at every turn.

The two snakes then confront each other, raising their heads and the front third of their bodies in threat. Despite such aggression, they do not bite their rivals.

When an adder is about to strike, its mouth opens almost 180 degrees. The fangs swing forward and muscles compress the venom glands to squeeze poison down a duct and through a channel to the tip of each fang.

DARK ADDERS

Adder markings can vary considerably and each animal has its own distinguishing pattern. In some individuals, the upper surface may be black or dark brown, known as melanism (as opposed to albinism, where the creature is white). Such animals are rarely completely black and usually have whitish dots on the lips, reddish markings on the throat, or a yellow tip to the underside of the tail. Zigzag markings are often still visible. Black adders are especially numerous in the New Forest and on the Gower peninsula of south Wales.

Very dark adders are not uncommon, although almost totally black adders on which no zigzag marking can be discerned, like this individual, are much rarer.

tissues begin to break down straight away, so the adder's meal is effectively semi-digested even before it is swallowed. Baby adders are just as capable of delivering a venomous bite as an adult.

Scare tactics
An adder is helped in its attempts to escape trouble – which it will always try to do – by its dramatic skin pattern. This disguises its outline, camouflaging it from predators as well as prey. If confrontation is unavoidable, the adder will first threaten potential enemies rather than attacking them. If this fails, it may produce a distinctive, musky odour from its anal gland and is likely to give a warning hiss, especially if it is a pregnant female. The snake usually makes the sound by exhaling air but can also hiss

when inhaling. Its enemy may take heed and back off, allowing the adder to escape, but if not, the snake may bite.

Venom is a vital commodity for the adder, essential for it to obtain food, so is not to be wasted on defence unless the snake is cornered, tormented or trodden on. So although an adder may sometimes deliver a venomous bite to defend itself, it can also bite without using its fangs. Around 70 per cent of adder bites on people are 'dry', with no venom being injected. Even a full bite is rarely fatal to a healthy adult. Records suggest that only 14 deaths have occurred in Britain over the last century. The risk of dying from an adder bite is far less than the risk of dying from a bee or wasp sting, which, together with other insects, cause roughly 60 fatalities in Britain each decade.

Despite its various defence tactics, the adder does fall prey to a number of predators. Buzzards are particularly adept at catching snakes, while small adders may be taken by frogs, toads, sand lizards and shrews. Adult adders are sometimes eaten by smooth snakes, as well as by various birds of prey, herons, owls, crows, ravens, magpies, gulls, and even pike and eels. Foxes, wild cats, rats and hedgehogs may also kill and eat adders.

Other causes of adder mortality include road traffic, dogs and cats, persecution by man and fire, to which heathland adders are particularly prone. Around 24 per cent of adders die annually – mainly through deliberate or accidental killing by humans – and 88 per cent of juveniles will not live to be three years old. With luck, however, a wild adder may live for up to ten years.

Weaving and swaying against each other in a strange dance, the males both attempt to push their rival to the ground. Eventually one, usually the intruder, becomes exhausted and retreats, leaving the victor to mate with the female.

Prey such as this wood mouse is swallowed head first. The snake drags the body into its throat by working each side of its loosely hinged, wide-opening jaws independently. Meanwhile, its throat stretches wide to engulf the prey.

Adders mate in spring, their bodies entwined to assist in the process. Females are usually larger than males and reddish or brownish; males are paler, like this one with a cream ground colour.

DANGER!

If you are bitten by an adder, you should try to stay calm, rest the affected area or immobilise it with a splint or bandage. Do not make incisions, apply suction or tourniquets, or otherwise try to treat the bite yourself. Seek medical help immediately.

Winter refuge

In late September or October, adders seek out cool, dry burrows or other sheltered places in which to hibernate. These dens are usually situated on elevated, south-facing, open banks that are free from flooding and frost, and are often found beneath exposed tree roots, inside rabbit or other mammal burrows, or old anthills. Man-made structures, such as rock piles, building foundations and stacks of straw, are also sometimes used. A good den is often shared by several snakes, sometimes in large groups of a dozen or more. The den is then known as a hibernaculum – one in Finland reputedly contained an astonishing 800 adders. These winter dens may even be shared with hibernating lizards, frogs, toads and newts – potential prey – but the snakes are sluggish on awakening and unlikely to attack.

Male adders retire to hibernate earlier than the females and emerge first in the spring, in late February. Once they leave their hibernation dens, the snakes remain in the general vicinity until they have mated. After mating, they travel up to 2km (1¼ miles) to damper areas with denser vegetation and in hot summers they particularly favour cool, marshy ground. Unlike grass snakes, however, adders are not water lovers – although they are able to swim if necessary.

Summer warmth

As a reptile, the adder relies on the heat of the sun to raise its body temperature to the point where it can become active enough to feed and mate. Adders like to be warmer than either of the other two British snake species – the grass snake and smooth snake – and spend a lot of time basking. When an adder emerges in the morning, it orientates itself at right angles to the sun and expands its ribs outwards to flatten its body and expose the maximum area to the warmth. It is the only British snake to do this habitually.

Adders are usually awake when the air temperature rises to 10–13°C (50–55°F), but they become active only at a body

SHEDDING SKIN

As an adder grows, it sheds or 'sloughs' its skin at intervals and grows a slightly larger one. This allows the snake to get bigger and also replaces any damaged portions of skin. The frequency of moulting depends on the weather, especially the temperature and how well fed the animal is.

Before the moult, the snake's eyes begin to appear foggy as the skin covering them loosens, and its body becomes duller and darker. The skin is freed with the help of a lubricating fluid, and peels off – usually in one piece – as the adder squeezes between grass stems or twigs, preferably in moist conditions. Only the thin, outermost layer of scales and skin is shed, so there is no blood. The moulted skin is semi-transparent, but still shows faint traces of the zigzag markings. Sloughed adder skin was once believed to have medicinal properties, and was worn as a cure for rheumatism, sunstroke and headache.

The moulted skin is very thin, but it still shows the distinction between the small oval scales of the adder's back and the large scales that cover the belly.

temperature of 20°C (68°F). On windy days an adder may not emerge at all and in hot weather it may retreat under cover at midday. Warm mats of dead bracken are favourite basking sites.

Warmth increases muscle efficiency, accelerates digestion and is essential to the development of the sexual organs and embryos. Pregnant females therefore spend more time basking than males.

Courtship and mating

A few weeks after emerging from hibernation, male adders shed their skins and move to favoured basking sites to await the emergence of the females. Mating takes place in April and early May. The female produces a chemical signal, or pheromone, that makes the male travel alongside her, often for several hours at a time, lashing his tail and tapping his head along her back while flicking his tongue. This can go on for some days. The two rest between bouts of feverish activity, which are stimulated by another pheromone secreted from the female's skin.

The male has two hollow mating organs called hemipenes, which are normally held inside out within the base of his tail. When the female is receptive, the two lie together with their tails held erect, and the male inserts one of the hemipenes into her vent to transfer both his sperm and a substance that may seal her oviduct to prevent rival males mating with her subsequently. The pair may lie like this for up to two hours before separating.

Some weeks after mating, the female sheds her skin before moving to her summer feeding grounds. In late August

Young adders are independent from the day of their birth, but since they are born with a supply of nutrients they do not need to eat during the three to six weeks before entering hibernation.

or September she returns to her hibernation site, where over the following 12 days she gives birth to between three and 18 young.

The young adders are born with enough food, in the form of yolk, to keep them alive through the winter, and they do not start to hunt for themselves until the following spring.

Adders have several enemies, including humans, and if a snake feels threatened, it may feign death. This usually involves relaxing its body and flopping on its back, sometimes with gaping mouth and lolling tongue.

Recognising moorland butterflies

On a sunny day, colourful butterflies ranging from the common small heath to the scarce dingy skipper flutter over moors and heaths in search of nectar-rich flowers.

Warm, dry heathland is particularly favoured by butterflies. Moorland is usually wetter and colder, even in summer, so is a more difficult habitat for them, but it nevertheless supports a variety of species, depending on the availability of food plants.

Some butterflies found in other habitats also live on moors and heaths. Painted ladies, for instance, are generally thought of as garden butterflies, yet great numbers can be seen on dry heathland when they arrive from continental Europe in spring.

Moorland residents

So long as there is sufficient warmth from the sun, brown butterflies, such as the small and large heath, are likely to be on the wing. They are constantly seeking nectar-rich flowers, such as thistles and brambles, and looking out for potential mates. The main reason they frequent moor and heath is that their larvae feed on various grasses growing there.

Two other browns, the grayling and the wall brown, are butterflies of stony, open sites. The grayling has a jerky flight and may be seen inland on heaths and downs, as well as among dunes or under cliffs along the coast. It often rests on patches of bare earth, where the mottled brown undersides of its wings provide excellent camouflage.

The wall brown (or wall) is scarcer, taking its name from its habit of basking on the tops of walls and rocky outcrops.

More eye-catching than the browns, the fritillaries are also commonly seen on heaths and downs on calm sunny days. During overcast or windy weather they are likely to hide deep among vegetation, making them almost impossible to see, despite their bright colours. In places, the pearl-bordered fritillary may be found on bracken-covered hillsides and the marsh fritillary on damp moorland.

The hairstreaks provide interest throughout the milder months of the year. By far the earliest member of the group to emerge is the green hairstreak, which may be seen flying in mid-April in mild years, although May and June are more typical. This species is common in many parts of the British Isles, from southern heaths to Scottish moorlands.

Purple hairstreaks prefer oak scrub. During a warm, still late afternoon in July or August, clouds of these beautiful butterflies may be seen on the wing, flying around the tops of the trees.

Threatened habitats

All butterfly species are sensitive to habitat change and the effects of modern farming practices. Over the past 150–200 years, five British butterfly species have become extinct, while others are becoming increasingly rare. For example, the dark brown dingy skipper has declined seriously in recent years. It is very scattered, but may still be found in open dry heathland, where it favours a mix of bare ground for basking and tallish vegetation on which to settle.

The green hairstreak is hard to spot because the colour of its underwings is a good match for the leaves on which it rests.

EASY GUIDE TO SPOTTING MOORLAND BUTTERFLIES

WHAT ARE MOORLAND BUTTERFLIES?

● All butterflies belong to the order Lepidoptera.

● Most species of brown butterfly, a subgroup of the family Nymphalidae, have an underwing pattern similar to that of the upperwing, although it is generally paler. The wings are mostly brown with eyespots.

● The fritillaries, another subgroup of the family Nymphalidae, have orange-brown upperwings with black spots and lines. The underwings have intricate patterns, including silvery patches with a metallic sheen. Those that frequent moorlands are among the smaller fritillaries and have a relatively slow, graceful, gliding flight.

● Hairstreaks and blues, both from the family Lycaenidae, are relatively small and fly quite swiftly. Their wings have a metallic sheen. The caterpillars are often protected from predators by ants because the ants like to eat the caterpillars' sugary secretions.

Distribution map key

███ Present   ☐ Not present

WILDLIFE WATCH

Where can I see moorland butterflies?

● Visit moorland or heaths in sunny weather. On dull days, butterflies such as the hairstreaks may be found crawling sluggishly over low plants, but the fritillaries, blues and browns tend to remain hidden among the vegetation.

● The green hairstreak is found on heathland and moorland, as well as on downland, in open areas in woodland, and anywhere else that gorse and ling – its larval foodplants – thrive.

● The purple hairstreak is found among scrubby oak on heathland as well as around oak trees as far north as southern Scotland.

● The marsh fritillary frequents damp heathland where devil's-bit scabious grows.

● The silver-studded blue is found on many lowland heaths in southern England, including the New Forest in Hampshire and the borders of Surrey and Hampshire.

GREEN HAIRSTREAK *Callophrys rubi*

An extremely active little butterfly, the green hairstreak has uniformly brown upperwings apart from a tiny white scent patch on each forewing in males. Chrysalises of this species usually rest below ground, in black ants' nests, where they make clearly audible squeaking noises.

● SIZE
Wingspan about 30mm (1¼in)

● FOODPLANT FOR LARVAE
Bilberry, gorse and rock rose

● CHRYSALIS
Rounded, squat and greenish brown; usually below ground

● ADULT SEASON
May–June

● HABITAT
Heaths, commons and gorse-covered coastal slopes

● DISTRIBUTION
Widespread throughout mainland but scattered in southern Scotland and Ireland

The green hairstreak is the only member of the family Lycaenidae that does not have tail streamers.

Upperwings brown (females paler than males)
Antennae and legs banded black
Underwings bright metallic green
Curved line of white dots on hind wing

SILVER-STUDDED BLUE *Plebeius argus*

The male silver-studded blue has violet-blue upperwings with a white border. The female has brown upperwings with creamy buff markings near the outer edges. The underwings of both sexes are grey with orange and black spots. Its small size makes this butterfly difficult to follow in flight.

● SIZE
Wingspan about 28mm (1⅛in)

● FOODPLANT FOR LARVAE
Gorse, ling and bell heather

● CHRYSALIS
Green, found below ground, often in black ants' nests

● ADULT SEASON
July–August

● HABITAT
Mainly open heathland

● DISTRIBUTION
Heaths in southern England; occasionally farther north

On heathland the silver-studded blue is associated with heathers or gorse. Where its foodplants remain, it can be common.

Male's upperwings are blue
Blue area indicates underwing of male. Female's is duller and greyer
Upperwings have white margins and a thick dark inner border
Underwings greyish with rows of dark spots and orange crescents

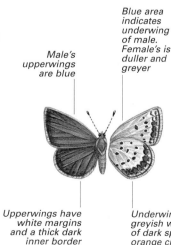

SMALL PEARL-BORDERED FRITILLARY *Boloria selene*

The underwings of this attractive butterfly distinguish it from its close relative, the pearl-bordered fritillary. The hind wings of both have a row of 'pearls' around the edge but in the small species they are framed in black (not red). Bracken-covered south-facing slopes are a favourite haunt.

● **SIZE**
Wingspan about 40mm (1⅝in)

● **FOODPLANT FOR LARVAE**
Violets

● **CHRYSALIS**
Brown and sculptured with silver spots; suspended from leaf stalk

● **ADULT SEASON**
June–early July

● **HABITAT**
Moorland and damp grassland in north and west; open, deciduous woodland in south

● **DISTRIBUTION**
Widespread but localised

In dull weather this butterfly often allows a close approach when it has settled, displaying its underwings.

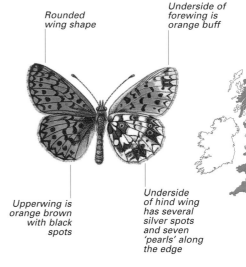

Rounded wing shape

Underside of forewing is orange buff

Upperwing is orange brown with black spots

Underside of hind wing has several silver spots and seven 'pearls' along the edge

SMALL HEATH *Coenonympha pamphilus*

An orange-brown butterfly with an eyespot on the under surface of the mainly orange forewing, the small heath is common on chalk downs and in many areas of grassland, but absent from other seemingly suitable areas. It is active only in sunny weather.

● **SIZE**
Wingspan about 35mm (1⅜in)

● **FOODPLANT FOR LARVAE**
Fine-leaved grasses

● **CHRYSALIS**
Suspended from grass stems in low vegetation

● **ADULT SEASON**
Late May–mid-July; second brood August–September

● **HABITAT**
Grassy heaths, downs and dunes

● **DISTRIBUTION**
Widespread but more common in south

Small heaths rest with their wings held vertically. The forewings are tucked behind the hind wings at night.

Upperwings mainly orange brown

Pattern on under surface of forewing similar to upper surface, but with pale whitish-grey margin

Large eyespot

Under surface of the hind wing marbled pale greyish brown

LARGE HEATH *Coenonympha tullia*

One of the most variable species in the British Isles, there are three forms of large heath. In the far north of Scotland it has mainly pale greyish wings with virtually no eyespots. Farther south, the wings are darker and smaller with distinct eyespots. In lowland England the wings are a brighter, reddish orange with bold eyespots.

● **SIZE**
Wingspan about 38mm (1½in)

● **FOODPLANT FOR LARVAE**
Mainly hare's-tail and cotton-grass

● **CHRYSALIS**
Suspended from low vegetation

● **ADULT SEASON**
Late June–early August

● **HABITAT**
Moorland, raised and blanket bogs mainly below 500m (1640ft)

● **DISTRIBUTION**
Central Wales northwards and Ireland

Moorland plants, including heather, provide cover for large heaths. Like the small heath, this species always rests with its wings folded.

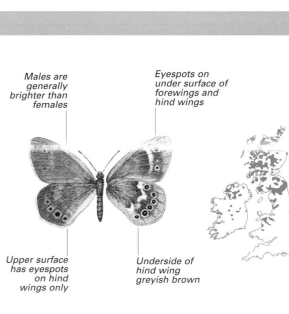

Males are generally brighter than females

Eyespots on under surface of forewings and hind wings

Upper surface has eyespots on hind wings only

Underside of hind wing greyish brown

Heaths and heathers

When summer draws to a close, a spectacular floral display reaches its peak on heathland and moorland as heathers open in a profusion of pink, white and purple blooms.

A group of low-growing shrubs of the family Ericaceae, heaths and heathers are so commonly found on lime-poor soils that their favourite habitat has been named after them – heathland. Some species prefer well-drained land and others boggy sites but, in either case, a fungus grows within their roots, enabling the plants to absorb nutrients from the often peaty earth.

Common sight
Heather, bell heather and cross-leaved heath are major features of these landscapes. Huge areas of moorland in the north and west of Britain, for example, are covered in heather. However, various other species of heath are less well known. They occur in a small number of specific sites, mainly in south-western England and western Ireland, especially near coasts.

Heather or ling (*Calluna vulgaris*) and heaths (*Erica*) are evergreen plants with very small, narrow leaves, which mostly curl inwards at the edges. Heath leaves are especially needle-like and mostly arranged in whorls of three to six along the stem, while heather leaves are attached in two opposite rows.

The flowers of both are small (although heath flowers are larger than heather's) and massed in heads or spikes, usually two to nine in a loose cluster. They are whitish, pink, lilac or purple in colour. Each flower is a hanging, bell-shaped inflated tube of fused petals, narrowed at the end, with the opening flanked by four lobes. Each flower is surrounded by four sepals (outer flower parts), which are longer than the petal tube in heather, shorter in the heaths.

Enclosed by the petals are eight, sometimes ten, male pollen-producing filaments (stamens) and a long, slender female one (style). The fruit is a capsule, which splits when ripe. The production of copious nectar attracts large numbers of pollinating bees in summer.

Traditional uses
Heather has had many uses over the years. It was always important as a forage plant on areas of marginal land, although today the regular grazing that once kept the heathlands of southern England free of scrub and trees has more or less stopped. In highland areas, heather was

Bell heather is abundant in the north and west and on the heaths of southern England. It flowers from July to September and is distinguished by its glossy, dark green leaves and purple flowers.

once used for bedding and for thatch. It still provides a major source of nectar for honeybees, and was at one time brewed into a type of beer.

Heather moors support a number of birds, such as red grouse, merlin and hen harriers. Red grouse, which are not found in any other environment, feed mainly on the young shoots.

Native heather and heaths are popular, hardy plants, and their hybrids and cultivars (cultivated varieties) are widely grown for ornament in parks and gardens.

HEATH AND HEATHER FACT FILE

● **Ling or heather**
Calluna vulgaris
Habitat and distribution
Heaths, moors, open birch, oak and
pine woods, drier bogs, coastal cliffs
and lime-poor sand dunes
Size 10–60cm (4–23½in) tall
Key features
Compact dwarf shrub, the lower stems
becoming quite woody; leaves 1–2cm
(½in) long, dense, overlapping in 4 rows,
sometimes with grey down; flowers tiny,
conspicuously four-lobed, pale purple
(rarely white), massed in branched spikes
Flowering time
July–September

● **Bell heather**
Erica cinerea
Habitat and distribution
Drier heaths, moors and coastal cliffs
Size 40cm (16in) tall
Key features
Compact dwarf shrub; numerous leaves,
narrow, spreading, hairless, dark green or
bronze in groups of 3; flowers 4–6mm
(⅛–¼in) long, bright crimson-purple, in long
spikes or clusters; stamens not protruding
Flowering time
June–September

● **Cross-leaved heath**
Erica tetralix
Habitat and distribution
Wet heaths, moors and bogs
Size 50cm (20in) tall

Key features
Similar to bell heather, but leaves greyish
and downy in groups of 4; flowers
5–9mm (¼–⅜in) long, pale rose-pink in
short clusters
Flowering time
June–October

● **Mackay's heath**
Erica mackaiana
Habitat and distribution
A few blanket bogs in west Galway and
Donegal, Ireland
Size Up to 60cm (23½in) tall
Key features
Similar to bell heather, but leaves broader
and edged with hairs in groups of 4;
flowers purplish-pink, in shorter, more
compact clusters
Flowering time
August–September

● **Dorset heath**
Erica ciliaris
Habitat and distribution
Damp heaths in Dorset, south Devon and
especially Cornwall, also one area of
blanket bog in County Galway, Ireland
Size 60cm (23½in) tall
Key features
Similar to bell heather, but taller and less
compact; leaves more oval, fringed with
long hairs; flowers 8–12mm (⅜–½in) long,
in reddish pink spikes
Flowering time
May–October

Bell heather
Erica cinerea

Cross-leaved heath
Erica tetralix

Mackay's heath
Erica mackaiana

Dorset heath
Erica ciliaris

Ling or heather
Calluna vulgaris

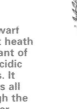

**The dwarf
Dorset heath
is a plant of
wet, acidic
heaths. It
flowers all
through the
summer.**

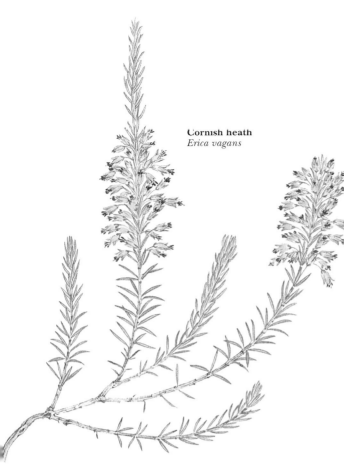

Cornish heath
Erica vagans

● **Cornish heath**
Erica vagans
Habitat and distribution
Abundant on coastal heaths on Lizard
Peninsula, Cornwall and at one site in
County Fermanagh, north-west Ireland
Size 30–80cm (12–32in) tall
Key features
Sprawling; leaves in groups of 4 or 5;
flowers 2.5–3.5cm (1–1⅜in) long,
purplish, lilac or pink, with darker,
purplish-brown tops of stamens
protruding, massed in long, dense,
leafy spikes
Flowering time
July–September

● **Irish heath**
Erica erigena
Habitat and distribution
Wet moors and bogs in County Mayo,
Ireland, extending to west Galway
Size 0.3–2m (1–6ft) tall
Key features
Erect branches; leaves hairless in
groups of 4; flowers 5–7mm (¼in) long,
pale pinkish-purple, with reddish-
brown tops of stamens slightly
protruding in a dense, leafy spike
Flowering time
March–May

● **Portuguese heath**
Erica lusitanica
Habitat and distribution
Naturalised on railway embankments
and heaths in Cornwall and Dorset
Size Up to 1–3m (3–9ft) tall
Key features
Tall with erect branches; leaves
hairless, light green, in groups of 3–5;
flowers 4–5mm (⅛in) long, white (pink
in bud), in leafy spikes; dark reddish
stamens large and barely protruding
Flowering time
January–May

● **Blue heath**
Phyllodoce caerulea
Habitat and distribution
Very rare plant of rocky moorland in
part of Perthshire and Inverness
Size 5–20cm (2–8in) tall
Key features
Small undershrub with narrow,
crowded leaves; flowers 7–12mm
(¼–½in) long, lilac or pinkish purple,
small clusters of 2–6, similar to those
of bell heather, but larger, paler and
drooping on slender, hairy stalks
Flowering time
June–July

● **St Dabeoc's heath**
Daboecia cantabrica
Habitat and distribution
Common in places on moors, heaths
and rocky ground from Connemara in
County Galway to County Mayo
Size Up to 50cm (20in) tall
Key features
Undershrub with a loose, untidy
growth; leaves alternate rather than in
whorls, spear-shaped, green and shiny
above, whitish beneath; flowers
9–14mm (⅜–⅝in) long, 3 in a long,
loose cluster, larger than those of
other heathers
Flowering time
May–September

**Cornish heath is naturally confined
to a small area of western Cornwall
and a single site in Ireland, but it is
also cultivated in gardens, from
which it occasionally escapes.**

Portuguese heath
Erica lusitanica

St Dabeoc's heath
Daboecia cantabrica

Blue heath
Phyllodoce caerulea

Irish heath
Erica erigena

Moorland grasses

On moors everywhere, grasses flourish. Together with their sedge and rush relatives, they are as varied as the types of soil in which they take root and for a few months every year, the subtle colours of their flowers enhance the wild landscape.

Take a bracing walk on a windswept moor at any time of year and the chances are that if the predominant plant is not heather, it will be grass – in summer forming a living carpet with green, purplish or brownish flowers rolling away across the hills into the distance. Grasses mingle with sedges, rushes and wood-rushes, depending on the nature of the underlying rock, type of soil, its fertility, climate, aspect (for example, south-facing or north-facing) and altitude.

In the drier, more fertile areas of moorland the dominant grasses are often sheep's fescue and common bent, or sometimes creeping bent. Where soil conditions are more acidic, other species are likely to be found, notably heath grass, wavy hair-grass and heath wood-rush.

In areas where grazing by livestock is heavy, the tastier fescues and even the less palatable bents are gradually eliminated. The resultant absence of competition between such species allows another grass, mat-grass, to gain a hold. This is much tougher and less nutritious to livestock than the fescues and bents, so it is not grazed so heavily. With the reduction in grazing, the mat-grass takes over. This type of grassland is found on moorlands between 300 and 600m (1000 to 2000ft), where rainfall is higher, the soil more acidic and the plant species less diverse than in lower, more fertile locations.

Natural cover
Purple moor-grass is very common in western parts of the British Isles, where it grows mainly on the damp, peaty

soils that lie between dry and boggy areas of moorland. In the bogs, purple moor-grass has adapted to cope with the wetter conditions, becoming smaller and non-tufted, and this species is often found growing side by side with deer-grass and the shrub bog myrtle.

Wavy hair-grass and heath rush (or moor rush) may crop up amid the purple blooms on heather moorland. On the wettest parts of the moor, where *sphagnum* moss proliferates on the waterlogged soils that cover less porous rocks, deer-grass, purple moor-grass and cotton-grasses all thrive.

High altitudes and mountain summits favour woolly hair-moss, an alpine heath species. When this moss decays, it produces humus – organic matter that fertilises the soil – which builds up and

creates conditions in which viviparous fescue grass, a non-flowering species, takes over.

Grazing sheep
Grassy moors are of great importance to upland farming, especially in providing fodder for sheep. Unfenced flocks grazing the moors – or sheepwalks, as these areas are called – are features of the upland landscapes of Dartmoor and Exmoor, many of the Welsh mountains, the fells of the Lake District, the Pennine hills, the Cheviots, the southern uplands, and the southern and western Highlands of Scotland, as well as much of the higher ground in Ireland.

Common bent grass dominates large expanses of moorland. Its flowers and fruits are borne in open branched clusters.

MOORLAND GRASSES FACT FILE

● **Heath grass**
Danthonia (Sieglingia) decumbens
Habitat and distribution
Dry, acidic moorland, also on heaths and other grassland with similar conditions; Most common on moorlands in south-west England, Wales, northern England, Scotland and Ireland
Size 5–60cm (2–23½in) tall
Key features
Low-growing, often almost prostrate, in dense tufts; leaves pale green, often with sparse hairs, and with a dense ring of hairs where they join the stem; flower spikelets almost globular, each with 4–6 flowers
Flowering time
June–August

● **Wavy hair-grass**
Deschampsia flexuosa
Habitat and distribution
Dry moors, heaths, woods on acidic soils; most common in south-west England, Wales, northern England and Scotland
Size 20–100cm (8–40in) tall
Key features
Leaves green, thread-like, with short, blunt membranes (ligules) where the leaves join the stems; flower spikelets shining silvery purplish, with awns (extensions of scales making up flowers) long and bent
Flowering time
May–July

● **Heath wood-rush**
Luzula multiflora
Habitat and distribution
Moorland and heaths on acidic soils, common in southern England, Wales, northern England, Scotland, and western and northern Ireland
Size 20–30cm (8–12in) tall
Key features
Tufted growth; leaves green, covered with long, white hairs; flowers on stalks in erect branched clusters, reddish brown, with anthers (pollen-carrying tip of stamen) the same length as flower-stalks; fruits globular, brown
Flowering time
May–June

● **Mat-grass**
Nardus stricta
Habitat and distribution
Very infertile soils on moors, mountains and heaths, particularly Exmoor, Dartmoor, Wales, northern England, Scotland and north-west Ireland
Size 10–20cm (4–8in) tall
Key features
Leaves wiry, greyish-green; flower spikes one-sided, with a single flower in each spike; outer scale (lemma) of each flower has only a short awn (extension of flower scale)
Flowering time
June–August

● **Heath rush (or moor rush)**
Juncus squarrosus
Habitat and distribution
Moors and heaths on acidic soils, scarce or absent in much of England but quite common in Wales, much of northern England, Scotland and northern Ireland
Size 15–50cm (6–20in) tall
Key features
Grows in tufts with a basal rosette of wiry green leaves; stems very stiff and usually leafless bearing branched cluster of flowers part way up; flowers dark brown with pale edges; fruits brown, egg-shaped
Flowering time
June–July

WILDLIFE WATCH

Where can I see moorland grasses?

● Any area of relatively dry moorland that is not managed as a heather moor is likely to be clothed in grasses, with sedges and rushes in the wetter parts.

● The Cairngorms region of the Scottish Highlands is a very good place to see grasses, sedges and rushes

● Cotton-grasses, which are at their best during summer when they turn patches of boggy ground white with their nodding fruiting heads, must be sought out in the wettest areas.

Wavy hair-grass
Deschampsia flexuosa

Heath wood-rush
Luzula multiflora

Heath grass
Danthonia (Sieglingia) decumbens

Heath rush
Juncus squarrosus

Mat-grass
Nardus stricta

**Common
cotton-grass**
*Eriophorum
angustifolium*

MOORLAND GRASSES FACT FILE

● **Purple moor-grass**
Molinia caerulea
Habitat and distribution
Common on moorland and wet heaths on
acid soils throughout the British Isles
Size 15–100cm (6–40in) tall
Key features
Compact tufts of greyish-green leaves
form conspicuous, often large tussocks;
ring of hairs where leaves join stem;
flower clusters narrow, with each spikelet
made up of 1–4 flowers, usually purple,
occasionally yellow or green, with purplish
brown anthers
Flowering time
July–September

● **Deer grass**
Trichophorum cespitosum
Habitat and distribution
On acidic moors, bogs and heaths, most
commonly in northern England, the
Scottish Highlands, and northern and
western Ireland
Size 5–35cm (2–14in) tall
Key features
Sedge with tufts of erect, rounded stems,
sometimes forming conspicuous tussocks,
which are leafless except for a single short
strap-like leaf near the base; reddish brown
to yellowish flowers in solitary egg-shaped
spikelet at top of stem
Flowering time
May–June

● **Common cotton-grass**
Eriophorum angustifolium
Habitat and distribution
Commonest of four species of cotton-
grasses, this sedge is widespread on wet
peaty moorland and bogs on acid soil
Size 20–60cm (8–24in) tall
Key features
Stems smooth and three-sided at top only,
forming a point; leaves very narrow with
a long, three-sided tip and a short ligule
(membrane where leaf joins stem); flowers
brown with bright yellow anthers, appear in
spring in drooping clusters of spikelets;
fruiting heads (May–July) have noticeably
long white cottony hairs
Flowering time
April–May

● **Hare's-tail cotton-grass**
Eriophorum vaginatum
Habitat and distribution
Wet, peaty, acidic soils, especially blanket
bogs; most common in northern England,
Scotland and northern Ireland
Size 30–60cm (12–24in) tall
Key features
Easily distinguished from other cotton-
grasses by its single, erect flowering and
fruiting spikelet on long, rough stalk; forms
tussocks; three-sided leaves thread-like
Flowering time
June–October

● **Viviparous fescue**
Festuca vivipara
Habitat and distribution
High altitudes on moorland in Brecon
Beacons and Snowdonia, Wales, the Lake
District and Scotland, especially north-west
Highlands; also in parts of Ireland
Size 5–60cm (2–24in) tall
Key features
Grows in loose tufts, with wiry stems
and slender rhizomes; very similar to
sheep's fescue but instead of flower
spikelets has green shoots with reddish
sheaths at their bases
Flowering time
June–July

Deer grass
*Trichophorum
cespitosum*

Viviparous fescue
Festuca vivipara

Purple moor-grass
Molinia caerulea

Hare's-tail cotton-grass
Eriophorum vaginatum

Like the cotton-grasses,
deer grass is not a grass
but a member of the sedge
family. It often forms
conspicuous tussocks.

Upland watch

- The red deer
- The wild goat
- The red kite
- The peregrine falcon
- The crossbill
- The common lizard
- Recognising upland butterflies
- Upland orchids
- Insect-eating plants

The red deer

With the arrival of warmer weather, red deer move on to upland slopes, seeking fresh grass as well as new growth on trees and shrubs. Unlike some deer, they are both grazers and browsers and thrive on whatever food is available.

Ever since the ice retreated at the end of the last Ice Age, red deer have inhabited the forests and uplands of Britain. Once common, the population declined as the forests were systematically cleared for fuel and to make way for farmland and eventually housing, but recently this trend has been reversed. New forests of conifers have been planted, especially in Scotland, and the red deer is now more numerous than it has been for centuries.

Increasing numbers

The total British wild deer population probably exceeds 360,000. Around 95 per cent are in Scotland with a handful in Wales, and the rest scattered in various parts of England including Cumbria, the Pennines, Peak District, East Anglia and parts of the south-west. In Ireland, where it is uncertain whether the species is native or was introduced, about 800 red deer live in Killarney National Park in the south-west. On the other side of the country in Wicklow National Park, an introduced relative – the sika deer – has interbred with the red deer so extensively that no purebred red deer are left. Approximately 70,000 red deer are farmed in Britain and Ireland and 7500 or so are kept in deer parks where they can be watched at fairly close quarters.

Red deer are essentially forest animals but are highly adaptable and thrive on moorland and in upland hill country. Where food and cover are in good supply, densities can often exceed 15 per square kilometre (under half a square mile).

Feeding habits

Red deer are active throughout both day and night, resting and taking short naps when they can. Their days are divided by between five and nine feeding cycles.

◀ Red deer are adaptable animals. When good-quality grass is not available, they will browse on leaves and shoots from trees and shrubs.

▲ The dappled coat of a young red deer calf ensures excellent camouflage among the low vegetation of the forest floor.

RED DEER FACT FILE

The largest native wild land mammal in the British Isles, red deer are partially protected. For much of the year, adults live in single-sex herds, the males (stags) staying away from the females (hinds) and their young (calves).

● **NAMES**
Common name: red deer
Scientific name: *Cervus elaphus*

● **HABITAT**
Forests and woods, especially conifer plantations in Scotland; open hillsides (including heather moorland) especially in Scotland and the Pennines

● **DISTRIBUTION**
Most of Scotland, including most of the islands, south-west England, Cumbria and parts of East Anglia; small numbers in the New Forest and other parts of southern England; parts of Ireland; commonly kept in deer parks

● **STATUS**
Total British wild population more than 360,000 plus more than 800 in Ireland

● **SIZE**
Length of stags averages 200cm (6½ft); tail 20cm (8in); height 110cm (3½ft) at the shoulder, hinds are about 10% smaller; stag weight up to 190kg (419lb), hind weight up to 115kg (254lb)

● **KEY FEATURES**
Stags have large, branched antlers. Coat is dark reddish brown in summer with cream underbelly, rump and inner thighs; darker brownish or greyish winter coat. Short tail is a distinctive beige above creamy buff rump patch with no black outline

● **HABITS**
Lives in small herds; stags form sociable groups in spring while regrowing antlers, but become deadly rivals when the rut begins in late September; hinds solitary when giving birth but gather into herds with their offspring and the non-breeding males

● **VOICE**
Loud bellowing roars uttered by stags in the rut (mating season); hinds make a soft mooing sound to their calves and both sexes emit a sharp bark when alarmed; otherwise normally silent; vision and scent more important than sound for communication

● **FOOD**
Plants including grass and leaves; where good grazing/browsing is not available, coarse grasses, heather, dwarf shrubs and other substitutes, which are less nutritious and often result in increased tooth wear; tree bark, especially in winter, when snow covering the ground may also force them to raid farm crops

● **BREEDING**
Rutting late September to end October; births May–June; usually a single calf, but very occasionally twins where food supply is good

● **YOUNG**
Rufous coat with white spots, which disappear within a few weeks of birth

Older stags have the largest antlers since the number of branches increases with each season. The antlers are rounded in cross-section.

The bright reddish brown summer coat gives this deer its common name.

The ears are disproportionately large in order to pick up the slightest sound of danger. The sense of smell is also keen.

Distribution map key

 Present all year round

Not present

PROTECTED!

Red deer are protected during the summer by a closed hunting season. The precise dates are different in Scotland from those that apply in England and Wales.

After eating, the deer lie up somewhere safe to chew the cud. This is an effective way of digesting leaves and grass whereby the food is regurgitated and chewed for a second time. Once the process is complete, the deer venture out to feed again. This routine ensures that they spend just a short time in the open before returning to the safety of tree cover.

In deer parks, grazing by deer can cause damage to trees. The deer like to nibble at the leaves, creating a 'browse line', and young trees need to be protected from them. In the wild, the deer are not confined so do not attack all the trees so voraciously. Nevertheless, they do have a serious impact, especially on native pine forests and young conifer plantations. Unless the deer are fenced out, which is expensive, they will nibble the young trees and stunt their growth.

The start of the rutting season is marked by stags uttering loud bellowing roars; the sound is sometimes referred to as 'belling'.

Sometimes a tree crop is ruined or the trees grow in distorted shapes. For this reason, deer are often culled by foresters. On major Scottish estates, deer stalking has been developed as a source of income over the last 150 years.

In parks, the deer are also culled each year to maintain a constant population. This entails shooting about 15 per cent of the animals. Without management, the deer quickly become too numerous for the park to support and many would starve during the winter when there is insufficient food available for them all.

This happens in hill country where the food supply is poor. Up to 65 per cent of calves may die during their first winter,

especially towards the end, before new plant growth has begun. If the weather is intensely cold, or if prolonged snow cover prevents access to food, the mortality rate will rise steeply. Adults are less affected, but older individuals with worn teeth may not be able to process their food properly and this reduces their chances of survival.

Mating rivalry

The ritual of red deer stags attracting hinds is the culmination of the deer's annual life cycle. The rut, as the mating season is called, begins in late September and peaks in mid-October. The stags move to the same area they have used in

READY FOR THE RUT

The whole point of the ritualised performance of rutting is to ensure that the maximum proportion of the population is fathered by the strongest males.

The top stags pay a high price. Once the rut begins, they cannot afford to rest or take time off for feeding. A lapse in attention by a breeding stag may allow any of his rivals to sneak in and steal one or more of his hinds. Mating can occur at any time of the day or night, so constant vigilance is necessary.

The stags need to keep bellowing out their challenge and call to females, as well as patrol the group to stop them straying. They also need to maintain their dark coat and the heavy

aroma that accompanies them by wallowing in mud and urine.

After a few weeks of such activity, the stags are pretty well worn out and may have lost over 20 per cent of their body weight. For this reason, the biggest stags stop rutting first, but by that time they will have mated with almost all the females in the

harem, so even if a younger animal then takes over the herd, he will father few or no calves since the hinds are already pregnant.

Most active stags will father about two dozen young in their lifetime, but their life span is likely to be shorter than that of the females, largely because of the stresses of the rut.

A successful stag will often attract a dozen or more hinds and he will have to be constantly alert to deter interloping males.

Outside the breeding season, males are quite at ease with each other and often form male herds.

Safety in numbers

Fresh new leaves are an irresistible temptation to these one-year old hinds. Deer tend to feed in groups, not only because the best food might be concentrated in one area, but also as a safety precaution. The more deer in a herd, the better the chances that any approaching danger will be detected.

Deer have a wide field of vision, thanks to a horizontally enlarged pupil. The eyes are widely spaced so that they can see in all directions except directly behind.

By living in herds, red deer can afford to spend more time feeding since there is always likely to be at least one pair of eyes looking out for danger.

This wild red deer calf will suckle milk from its mother for up to seven months. The mother identifies her baby by its unique scent.

previous years and each one attempts to gather as many hinds as possible by roaring loudly and actively herding the females. They compete to mate with as many hinds as possible and success depends upon establishing social status.

Social climbers

A deer's place in the social hierarchy is settled by the exhibition of various status symbols, notably the antlers. If possible, a stag will avoid using his antlers as weapons since a fight with a rival involves the risk of serious injury or death. So the animals attempt to bluff each other into admitting defeat. A stag will parade up and down, showing off his antlers, thick neck and dark colour. Other stags, particularly younger ones with smaller antlers, will often not even attempt a challenge.

An older, more confident animal might indulge in 'parallel walking', marching up and down alongside a dominant stag to see if he will give way. Each eyes the other and only when neither will back down does a physical tussle take place, with antlers locked together and each animal straining to throw the other off balance. Finally, one will concede defeat, leaving the other in sole possession of the harem.

Meanwhile, the hinds will be attracted to the stags that display the highest status, that is the ones that roar loudest and most often, and have the biggest antlers. Occasionally, an impressive stag may attract as many as 50 hinds.

Stags do not usually begin to rut until their fifth or sixth year. They may wander for several years before settling down in an area of around 200–400 hectares (500–1000 acres), returning each September to the place where they were first successful in attracting a harem. Typically, a stag may have three or four years of breeding. Hinds are less adventurous and tend to remain close to their birth place, moving around with the seasons as food becomes available.

Fit to breed

Where food is plentiful, in deer parks for example, the hinds can breed in the year following their birth. Where food is poor, breeding may be delayed for another year, possibly two. Similarly, while most hinds will breed every year, they will not do so if they are in poor condition and on open upland it is usual for a third of the females not to breed in any one year.

Pregnancy lasts around 250 days and usually results in the birth of a single calf although very occasionally, in forested areas with a good food supply, twins may be born. However, losses are high,

especially in hill country, where a female may manage to raise only four offspring in her entire lifetime of about ten years.

The young are mostly born between late May and mid June, with each hind retreating to a secluded spot to give birth alone. The mother has to double her intake of food in the early days to ensure her calf's rapid growth. She may need to wander up to a kilometre (over half a mile) away from the calf's hiding place to obtain the food necessary to keep up a good supply of milk – but she returns to feed her calf every two or three hours in the first few days. After that, the frequency of suckling gradually decreases.

▲ In deer parks, grazing by red deer results in trees developing a distinctive 'browse-line'. Leaves survive only above the height that the deer can reach.

◄ Despite their size, herds of red deer can be remarkably unobtrusive in woodland settings. The best views are often afforded when they cross woodland rides or clearings.

Displaying stags

For male red deer in the rutting season, the display of social status is all important. The rest of the year males can live amicably together, with little sign of competition.

The angle of the head, held high, and thickness of neck are important in the body language of rutting red deer stags.

In the run-up to any fight, stags engage in 'parallel-walking' during which they gauge one another's power and strength.

A young male is clearly intimidated by the confident stance of the dominant stag.

The calf is born fully furred with its eyes open and it can run surprisingly fast even when only a few hours old. However, if threatened, a calf stays absolutely still, relying on the camouflage of its white-spotted brown coat to protect it. In the past, wolves were the principal predator but they are now extinct in the British Isles. Occasionally, golden eagles are known to take very young calves.

After about a week, the calves join their mothers to form a herd, often with the young gathered together in a 'creche' where they spend their time leaping and playing among themselves.

A single calf is the norm. Rarely, twins may be born where there is a plentiful supply of food, such as in a deer park.

Displays of status rarely result in physical battles. The subordinate animal usually concedes defeat without risking a real fight.

By challenging each other in the rut the stags ensure that only mature, fit males breed, which maintains the quality of the herd.

ANTLER GROWTH

When male red deer are a few months old, their antlers begin to grow. Each year in the spring – from mid March to the end of April – these are shed and replaced by a new set, bigger than the previous year's with the addition of an extra prong, called a tine, and covered by a fine furry skin called 'velvet'. The older stags shed their antlers first, and the number of tines does not always correspond exactly to the animal's age.

By the time the antlers reach their full size they are no longer encased in velvet, and the stags are ready for the rut.

A stag's antlers regrow annually inside a covering of fine fur.

WILDLIFE WATCH

Where can I see red deer?

● Deer parks are the best places to see red deer. Even rutting behaviour can be observed, with no risk of causing disturbance to the animals. Deer parks, such as Richmond Park in Surrey and Windsor Park in Berkshire, are often marked on road maps and may be associated with stately homes. Many National Trust properties have deer parks.

● Red deer may be observed in the wild in much of Scotland, especially the Highlands and Islands, on Exmoor (straddling the Devon-Somerset border), the Quantocks (Somerset) and in the New Forest (Hampshire). Wild deer are timid and should not be approached. In forested areas, the animals may be abundant but hard to see.

● Calves may be seen with their mothers in June and July, especially in deer parks.

● Always take care when watching red deer, especially in the rut when you should keep your distance and watch through binoculars. These large animals may attack intruding humans, causing serious injury.

The wild goat

Hardy and adaptable, goats are capable of surviving on a meagre diet. Their ability to scale rocky slopes and crags allows them to graze on vegetation that other animals cannot reach.

Goats were among the first animals to be domesticated, around 9500 years ago in the Middle East. They proved invaluable for their skins, milk and meat. Brought to Britain during the Neolithic period, their bones have been found dating back 4500 years. Over the centuries, escapees from domestic herds adapted to life in the wild and established their own feral groups. Today, their descendants still display characteristics of primitive ancient breeds, such as horns and upright ears, which have been lost in modern domestic goats.

Wild goats are agile creatures and most live on craggy cliffs and hillsides, often more than 300m (1000ft) above sea level. On such rough terrain, they are not a nuisance to farmers because crops are not grown there and goats are generally left

alone. In severe winters, they may have to retreat to lower levels, but they soon return to their favoured steep slopes and rocky ledges when the weather improves. Some herds share the same ground as sheep and the two species co-exist peacefully.

Hearty eaters

Goats will eat any vegetation that they can reach, but are especially fond of fresh grasses, leaves and sedges. In winter, they will eat shrubs, even prickly gorse. Unlike sheep, goats eat bracken and even small conifer trees. They may rear up on their hind legs to nibble leaves, something that sheep do not attempt.

The goat's complex digestive system requires the animals to consume large amounts of food and then rest while the

Undeterred by steep ground or broken, unstable terrain, wild goats venture on to high mountain slopes during the summer months. Family groups graze on the fresh growth of upland plants.

millions of microbes in their stomachs attack the plant material. Like sheep, goats are ruminants, periodically regurgitating a ball of semi-digested

DID YOU KNOW?

Goat horns have growth lines on them, just like the rings inside a tree. You can count these to determine the age of a particular animal. Ignore any fine lines, and count the large scars only. Most goats will be aged three years or under, but occasional individuals can live to more than ten years old.

WILD GOAT FACT FILE

The wild goat is a large and superficially sheep-like mammal with a shaggy coat that is often a mixture of black, grey and white. Small herds roam freely over moors and rocky hillsides, and along cliff tops, scaling near-vertical slopes with nonchalant ease.

● NAMES
Common names: wild goat, feral goat
Scientific name: *Capra hircus*

● HABITAT
Rocky mountainsides and steep slopes; open moorland and grassland; may move below 500m (1640ft) in harsh weather

● DISTRIBUTION
Scattered localities mostly in Scotland (two-thirds of population) but also along the England-Scotland border, in North Wales and a few places in south-west England; also on some islands

● STATUS
Total population around 3500

● SIZE
Height 60–70cm (2–2ft 4in) at shoulder; length 120–130cm (3ft 9in–4ft 4in); tail 10–12cm (4–5in); weight 25–65kg (55–145lb); males larger than females

● KEY FEATURES
Thick, hairy fur variably coloured; ears point directly upwards; both sexes have horns

● HABITS
Wary, active at night and during the day; lives in small herds

● VOICE
Bleating noises, especially by young; loud snort given as alarm call

● FOOD
Almost any edible plant material, including leaves, grass and bark

● BREEDING
Rut (mating season) in autumn; gestation period about 150 days. One or occasionally two kids born January–April (mainly March)

● YOUNG
Kids stay with mother for up to six months before becoming fully independent; often remain with same herd

● SIGNS
Droppings and footprints similar to those of sheep, but wild goat's toe prints splay out more at the tips

From an early age, kids practise the skills they will need as adults. Young males indulge in head-butting contests, a behaviour they will perform in earnest when they are sexually mature.

Distribution map key

![] Present all year round

![] Not present

Horns point upwards from the forehead and curve backwards. Older males have larger horns.

The thick coat insulates the goat from harsh upland winds.

Patches of hard, bare skin protect the forelimbs from knocks.

material and chewing it again, which is known as 'chewing the cud'. When the food is swallowed for a second time, it passes to further chambers before progressing to the true stomach and intestines. This complicated arrangement enables ruminants to consume food that would otherwise be indigestible.

During the summer, goats alternate between short periods of feeding and chewing the cud while during the winter months, they eat in the morning and ruminate while resting in the middle of the day.

Herd behaviour

In some places, the male goats, which are called billies, stay with the females, known as nannies, throughout the year, but elsewhere the billies live in small single-sex herds, tending to associate with those of similar age. In such bachelor herds, the oldest and biggest animals are dominant.

Males joust during the annual rut in an attempt to determine which billy is the strongest. The victor has first choice of mating the females in the assembled group.

Goats will eat woody vegetation and strip bark off trees, a type of feeding called browsing, which can be very destructive. However, browsing can be put to good use where woody scrub is a nuisance. Goats will eat the unwanted shrubs and help to create an open environment suitable for wild flowers and butterflies.

On Ventnor Down on the Isle of Wight, goats have successfully cleared an invasion of dense, non-native shrubs from the steep slopes. The plants would have been very difficult to remove by any other method. Now many native plants and animals have been restored to the area.

Wild goats have voracious appetites and are ingenious when it comes to devising ways of getting at hard-to-reach vegetation. They will rear up on their hind legs, stand on convenient rocky outcrops and even climb trees to feed.

▲ A male will often squirt his urine forwards so that it sprays on to his beard, scenting it strongly. He will then rub up against trees and rocks in his territory, transferring the unmistakable odour, so that other male goats are aware of his presence.

Nanny goats usually wander off alone to give birth to their young, known as kids, and then join other females to form small herds. Family groups of nannies and their offspring from the current and previous years tend to stick together and are occasionally joined by a billy.

The groups are led by the oldest female and have separate home territories. These may be small where food is plentiful but the average size is three square kilometres (just over a square mile). Sometimes the goats range over more than twice this area.

As the rut approaches in early autumn, larger groups may form, but the herds still comprise 8 to 15 animals only. At this time, billies disperse in search of females and social dominance is very important. High-ranking billies stare balefully at rivals until the rivals back down. If intimidation does not work, the billy lowers his head in an explicit threat. If this is also ignored, the two males ram their heads together, trying to take the blow on their horns and at the same time push their opponent off balance. Two stubborn billies, neither of which will give way, may spend several hours driving their heads together.

◄ For a male goat, part of the ritual of the rut involves trying to intimidate rivals. If the glaring eyes and aggressive posturing fail to impress, billies resort to head-butting to establish supremacy.

▼ Both male and female goats have horns that rise up from the forehead and curve backwards. Males have the largest horns, reaching an average of 39cm (15in) at three years and 75cm (30in) at 10 years.

Dominant billies regularly indulge in a pungent form of self-advertising by urinating on themselves. The strong smell ensures that inferior animals get wind of them early enough so they can flee and avoid a fight.

Young goats

Nannies usually give birth to one kid in March, five months after mating. Twins are uncommon and, if born, it is rare for both to survive. The newborn kid shelters in a small hideaway among rocks or in dense vegetation. Nowadays goats have little to fear from predators, since wolves are extinct and eagles are no longer widespread in Britain, but instinct ensures that the nannies look after their young by hiding them well. The female stays close to her offspring for several days. Gradually, she moves further away and soon the kid is able to follow her. Nannies continue to suckle their young for up to six months.

Kids are very vulnerable in the days following their birth. At least half of them die of starvation or disease before the end of summer. In severe or prolonged winters, the mortality rate may be high, wiping out almost all the young and several older animals as well. Milder winters mean that many more goats will survive. Provided the young goats get through their first winter, they can look forward to a relatively long life. Many live to be six or more years old, and some reach the grand old age of 10 years.

WILDLIFE WATCH

Where can I see wild goats?

● In Scotland, along the eastern side of Loch Lomond, goats live near Inversnaid Lodge and can be seen from the west Highland Way. Further north, they may be seen on the north side of Loch Morar, near Newtonmore on the A9 and also in the Findhorn Valley. Some goats live on the Mull of Kintyre and on several Scottish islands, including the Isle of Rhum National Nature Reserve. A wild goat park is situated between Newton Stewart and New Galloway on the A712.

● In England, wild goats can be seen at Brean Down in Somerset, at the Valley of the Rocks in north Devon, and on Lundy in the Bristol Channel. They also live in College Valley in Northumbria on Newton Tors.

● Wild goats live near the Llanberis Pass in Snowdonia in North Wales and are especially easy to see around the slate quarries of the Padarn Country Park. They also live at Cwm Bychan.

● The best sites to see wild goats in Ireland are the Wicklow Mountains, just 10km (6 miles) south of Dublin, and the Burren in County Clare.

The sure-footedness of the goat family is legendary. A goat will climb precipitous slopes and take death-defying leaps with absolute confidence.

The red kite

With the help of legal protection, the numbers of red kites are steadily growing, so the sight of these elegant birds twisting and turning effortlessly in the air is becoming more commonplace.

A hundred years ago the hills and valleys of mid-Wales were home to just one or two pairs of red kites. Today, more than 250 pairs breed there alongside numerous buzzards, ravens and a host of other wildlife, and new colonies have been established in other parts of Britain. Several conservation organisations, led by the Royal Society for the Protection of Birds (RSPB) and a number of government and other bodies, realised that Welsh kites were spreading very slowly despite a significant increase in their numbers. So birds from Spain and Germany were introduced to England and Scotland respectively and the breeding success of these new populations has been remarkable.

Ringing and wing tags have proved that the young from these releases cover wide areas in winter, as do some of the Welsh population, but they always return close to their release site to breed. One English bird was seen for two successive winters in Wales, but returned to England to nest.

Beautiful plumage

The red kite's rusty red body feathering, black-tipped wings, pale, dark-streaked, cream head and orange-red tail are striking, especially in good light, but its elegance becomes most apparent in flight. Its long wings and tail, combined with a lightweight body, make this bird of prey a superb and effortless flier.

Red kites often hang above hilltops, wings and tail flexing to maintain their position. This technique provides excellent opportunities for the birds to see even small items of food, such as earthworms, which form quite a large part of their diet in some places. They are mainly scavengers, however, and eat carrion wherever it is available. In the Cambrian Mountains in Wales, for instance, the carcasses of dead sheep are an important source of food.

Scavenging for food

On first sight of a carcass, the red kite is often wary, leaving magpies, carrion crows and buzzards to investigate.

Red kites nest in deciduous trees, sometimes adding to old crows' or buzzards' nests to make their own. Despite full legal protection and round-the-clock guarding in some cases, each year a few nests are robbed by egg collectors.

RED KITE FACT FILE

The bright rufous feathers on the adults' back and tail give this medium-sized, long-winged bird of prey its name. Its forked tail is particularly noticeable when the bird glides and soars.

● NAMES
Common name: red kite
Scientific name: *Milvus milvus*

● HABITAT
Upland, open country with patches of deciduous woodland

● DISTRIBUTION
Hills and valleys of mid-Wales; recently reintroduced to parts of Scotland, Yorkshire, the Midlands and Oxfordshire

● STATUS
Scarce but increasing; about 3000 birds

● SIZE
Length 60–66cm (2–2ft 2in); wingspan 140–165cm (4ft 7in–5ft 5in); weight 0.8–1.6kg (1lb 11oz–3lb 7oz)

● KEY FEATURES
Long wings, angled in flight; tail long, forked and russet; body colour varies from streaked pale buff in juveniles to streaked deep rusty red in adults; head pale; wings dark on underside except for pale (almost white) patch near tip; legs yellow

● HABITS
Adults very sedentary; young often wander many miles before returning to original territory to breed

● VOICE
High-pitched, thin whistle during breeding season and at communal feeding sites

● FOOD
Mostly carrion, especially dead sheep; meat left out at feeding stations; may kill small rabbits, voles, mice, young birds and invertebrates, especially earthworms

● BREEDING
March–July; replacement clutches rare

● NEST
Large, untidy nest of sticks, lined with sheep's wool or other soft material including paper, plastic or other rubbish; sited in fork of deciduous tree

● EGGS
2–3 white eggs, spotted with red; occasionally 4, or 1 if female is young; laid at intervals of 2–3 days; incubated by female for 31–32 days

● YOUNG
Naked at first; covered in down in 2–3 weeks; fledge in 7–9 weeks; may still be present at nest site in August

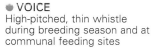

The red kite is given full legal protection by the Wildlife and Countryside Act 1981, Schedule 1. Intentional or reckless disturbance of breeding birds is an offence carrying a fine of up to £5000 and/or a prison sentence of six months.

The red kite has a buff-white head with darker streaks, piercing pale yellow eyes and a yellow bill with a black, hooked tip.

The body and inner wing feathers are rusty red.

The long wings have black tips on the upperside and pale patches near the tips on the underside.

The kite's long, forked tail is distinctive; no other large British bird has a tail like this.

Distribution map key

■ Present all year round

☐ Not present

Feathers that are moulted in spring are usually frayed at the tip, a sure sign they are worn out and in need of replacement.

KITE HISTORY

During the 12th and 13th centuries, red kites were regular scavengers of town and country, valued for the service they performed in removing carrion and rubbish. However, from the 16th century, various 'vermin acts' were passed and bounties were placed on the birds' heads. The species began a gradual decline in both numbers and territories. By 1880, kites had vanished from the whole of England and Scotland and their numbers were much reduced in Wales. By the end of the 19th century, the species was on the brink of extinction in Britain.

Until the mid-1930s, the population was reduced to one or two breeding pairs in the upper Tywi Valley, but since then, red kites have fared much better. The Kite Committee, founded in 1903, provided a degree of protection and by 1946 there was a slight increase to seven breeding pairs. From then on, there has been a steady increase, but it was not until the late 1980s that the number of breeding pairs exceeded 50. Today, there are five times that number in Wales.

Recovery was hampered by a lack of genetic diversity. Scientists at Nottingham University used genetic fingerprinting to show that up to 1977, the entire Welsh population of red kites was descended from a single female. Then in 1977, a female German kite arrived in Wales and joined the population, thus adding much needed genetic variety.

Soaring kites rarely fall victim to guns nowadays, but their scavenging habits still put them at risk from baited traps and poison-laced carcasses.

From below, the rust-coloured body and leading edge of the kite's inner wing contrast with the pale head and wing patches.

As the kite gains in confidence, it approaches cautiously, gradually gliding lower and lower. Eventually, in a sudden tumble, the kite drops down to feed, often attracting other kites in the process. The birds frequently utter high-pitched, whistling calls as they descend. The most dominant bird usually feeds first, even if it is not the first to arrive on the scene, while the others wait to take their turn.

Most birds of prey venture out only when they are hungry. The hunt is often brief and afterwards they usually return to the same branch, rock or cliff on which they have already spent many hours. Kites are more active than that and seem to spend longer flying, possibly because they are not so much predators as scavengers. Although red kites are not generally aggressive towards other birds of prey, they are adept at snatching food from them in flight, using their superior aerobatic skills to outmanoeuvre them. They also sometimes take mice, voles, young rabbits and birds, and even visit rubbish tips in search of food.

Breeding activity

Adult red kites usually begin to occupy their breeding territories around the beginning of March. The pairs soon start building or repairing old nests, and by the end of the month the first eggs are laid amid a warm lining of sheep's wool

or some other soft material. They have been known to use all kinds of artificial material to line their nests, including discarded plastic bags, rags, scraps of newspapers, pairs of tights and even children's toys.

The female incubates the eggs while the male keeps watch from nearby. His two main duties are to provide food for

the female and to chase off magpies, crows, ravens or other birds of prey, including rival red kites, that might steal the eggs. Occasionally, if the parents are alarmed – for instance, by people inadvertently wandering too close – they will both leave the nest, flying up high to watch proceedings, and an opportunist crow may slip in and steal an egg.

When foraging, red kites prefer extensive open areas with low vegetation where their prey is active and they can spot carrion easily. They either soar in swooping circles high in the air or fly low over the ground, flapping their strong wings slowly.

Mastery of the air

Slow-speed flight and superb aerodynamic control are the red kite's specialities. The large, broad wings that give it this ability would impede manoeuvrability if the bird did not have such a large and highly mobile tail.

Riding thermals – circling in a column of rising air – is the kite's preferred way of gaining height.

The kite strongly flexes its mobile tail to execute evenly paced, gentle turns.

As the bird glides, the wings are held slightly arched and kinked forwards and the tail is dipped in a shallow 'V'.

Aerial battles

When the eggs have hatched, the parents' work increases to provide for the young and also to keep other predators away. The aerial battles that take place during this period are fabulous to watch.

In one recorded example, a kite knew that a pair of peregrine falcons nesting about a mile away frequently stashed their leftovers a short distance from their own nest. The kite was aware exactly when the peregrines had finished feeding their young and hidden any remaining food.

Each time the kite entered the peregrines' air space, a superb aerial battle ensued. The peregrines would dive-bomb the intruder and the kite, with a sudden twist, would flip over on to its back to show its talons. As the peregrines pulled out of the dive, the kite plunged down to grab the leftovers. The peregrines continued their attacks for some distance, but the kite held on to the food and took it back to its young.

Downy chicks

The young generally remain in the nest for about eight weeks before they fledge. For the first two to three weeks they are brooded by the female to keep them warm, but after that time their covering of protective down has grown sufficiently for her to go off to collect food.

Nevertheless, weather can take its toll at this time. Strong winds or heavy rain can be fatal for newly hatched or very young chicks if they are left unattended by the parents for long.

A wide variety of food is brought to the nest, the majority of which is carrion.

Once carrion is sighted, a scavenging red kite may perch a short distance away to observe the scene before flying down to the carcass. On other occasions, it drops from a hunting perch to take live prey by surprise.

Spying from above

Long, broad wings and a relatively small body mass enable the red kite to stay airborne with very little forward movement. The hunter hangs in the air, raking the ground below with its piercing, yellow eyes for the sight of prey – alive or dead.

Perfect equilibrium in flight enables the tail to be used with maximum efficiency as both stabiliser and rudder.

On air currents rising from the hills below, the kite soars on stiffly held wings, its body completely still in relation to the ground.

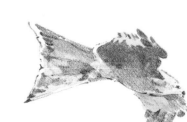

The red kite remains undetected by animals on the ground below.

THE RED KITE CALENDAR

JANUARY • FEBRUARY

Winter is a difficult time for kites in the uplands. Young birds may be some distance from their home territory. Hunting is difficult, which means the birds are attracted to regular feeding stations.

MARCH • APRIL

Adults return to their nests to rebuild them in readiness for egg laying, which usually begins in early April. Once the eggs are laid the birds remain with them. Disturbance at this critical time may result in desertion.

MAY • JUNE

The young hatch and are brooded by the female for the first two to three weeks. Males will be busy collecting food and chasing off other birds of prey and crows from the nesting area.

JULY • AUGUST

The young fledge, but stay close to the nest for a few weeks where both parents continue to supply food. At this time adults may moult, too, the feather loss producing some unusual-looking birds.

SEPTEMBER • OCTOBER

Young red kite are fending for themselves by now and often wander widely in search of regular feeding. This means that they can, and frequently do, turn up in some unexpected places far from home.

NOVEMBER • DECEMBER

Winter is a good time to see kites from the mountain roads in mid-Wales, with the numbers of birds swelled by the year's young. Many birds visit feeding stations at this time.

Animals that have been killed in road accidents provide a good source of food. Other items include nestling rooks and crows, as well as a few fish. The young develop fast on this high-protein diet and most fledge in mid-July.

The fledging season coincides with the time when farmers cut their fields for hay. Birds and small mammals may be killed in the process and red kites are to be seen following the mowing machines in search of sustenance. The young kites remain close to the nest for a while, but eventually fly away to establish their own territories. Most Welsh kites leave the valleys and head for the high ground of the Cambrian Mountains, where they feed on their usual carrion diet.

Feeding stations

With the onset of harsh autumn and winter weather, red kites tend to move back to lower ground but they may still make daily trips to upland areas to feed. At dusk in winter, they head to regular woodland roosting sites, where up to ten birds will occupy a single patch.

In Wales, well-established feeding stations enable more kites to survive severe winter spells than would be the case if they were left unaided. Snow can cover not only land but also potential food, and prolonged frosty weather can freeze sheep carcasses, making feeding difficult. Alternative food supplies have to be sought by the birds.

In Powys, the Rhayader kite feeding station, and another at nearby Tregaron, attract large numbers of kites and are popular with birdwatchers and tourists as well as the birds.

WILDLIFE WATCH

Where can I see red kites?

● Mid-Wales is the best place to see red kites, but breeding sites are kept secret to protect this sensitive species. At some kite centres, video links have been set up for enthusiasts to watch the birds in their carefully protected nest sites.

● Close views and marvellous aerobatic displays may be seen at kite feeding stations.

● Gigrin Farm, South Street, Rhayader, Powys (telephone 01597 810243) is signposted off the A470 about 1km (half a mile) south of the town centre. There are large hides and from 12 to as many as 30 kites visit each day. Feeding time is 3 p.m. in summer and 2 p.m. in winter; there is also a Kite Centre with a variety of displays.

● The Tregaron Kite Centre is located in the Old School House, Tregaron, Powys. Two or three places nearby may also be feeding kites. Ask Tregaron Kite Centre for information.

● The high roads through the Cambrian Mountains, such as the Elan Valley, are great for distant views of kites.

● In southern England, the Chilterns are a good place to see kites. They are regularly seen from the M40 (the driving should be delegated to someone who is not watching the kites).

● In Scotland, look around the Inverness area, including the Black Isle and Easter Ross. Further information, including a leaflet with a Red Kite Trail, is available from the North Kessock Tourist Information Centre beside the A9, just north of Inverness (telephone 01463 731505).

● The Welsh Kite Trust offers the chance to support research into red kites. Regular newsletters are issued detailing progress. Contact Tony Cross, Samaria, Nantmel, Llandrindod Wells, Powys, LD1 6EN (telephone 01597 860524).

In common with other day-flying birds of prey, the red kite has very keen eyesight. As it soars, it can spot potential food from long distances. It then swoops to seize small mammals or birds, or to claim the carcass of a dead animal, such as a rabbit.

A dead brown hare will attract a kite, which may first perch cautiously nearby or descend in ever-decreasing circles to settle on the ground next to the carcass.

The peregrine falcon

With its strong, hooked beak, keen eyesight and sharp talons, Britain's largest native falcon is a supreme hunter. Unparalleled speed and agility in the air make it the ultimate bird of prey.

Whether it is soaring high over open ground or gliding along a cliff face, the peregrine falcon is a master of the air. That effortless, graceful flight disguises the fact that the bird is moving at an average speed of 65km/h (40mph). Peregrines are often seen hunting over moorland and upland. They also inhabit coastal and wetland regions, where their hunting territories include beaches, cliffs, nearby farmland and the open sea.

A gliding peregrine makes a distinctive silhouette, resembling an anchor with its short tail and flat or slightly drooping wings, which span about 1m (3ft). The bird's pale breast is finely speckled. Its head is blackish on top and its face bears a characteristic broad black moustache that contrasts with its pale cheeks.

The peregrine's hunting technique begins with the bird circling up to several hundred metres high. Keeping its prey in its sights, the peregrine dives steeply, plummeting through the air at 250km/h (155mph) or more. If it brings its prey down, the peregrine may tear out the breast meat on the spot or take the carcass to a regular favourite perch, known as a plucking post. If no kill results, it may resume its high-altitude flight or retire to a high rocky ledge.

A powerful predator, the peregrine has large, forward-facing eyes for clear binocular vision, vital for accurately judging distances. This bird of prey can spot its quarry up to a kilometre away.

DID YOU KNOW?

Peregrine falcons have been used as hunting birds for millennia. There are references to falconry in Egyptian times. In the Middle Ages it was a favourite pastime of the nobility and peregrines were protected by royal decree. This was one of the first forms of legal protection for birds in Britain.

PEREGRINE FALCON FACT FILE

The peregrine falcon has a compact body shape, broad-based, pointed wings and a relatively short tail, which produces a distinctive silhouette in flight. When not hunting it flies effortlessly with a series of shallow flaps interspersed with glides.

● **NAMES**
Common name: peregrine falcon
Scientific name: *Falco peregrinus*

● **HABITAT**
Upland, coastal and wetland regions; expanding into new habitats such as cities

● **DISTRIBUTION**
Much of Wales, Scotland, Ireland (mainly along coast) and western England including Lake District, Pennines and south-west peninsula

● **STATUS**
Over 1400 pairs in UK, with an estimated 380 pairs in Ireland; recovered from a population low in the 1950s and 1960s

● **SIZE**
Length males 38–44cm (15–17⅜in), females 45–48cm (17¾–18⅞in); weight males 600–750g (21–26½oz), females 925–1300g (32½–45¾oz)

● **KEY FEATURES**
Large and stocky; sexes similar but female larger and usually with more white on upper breast; upperparts blue-grey, rump paler and wing tips darker; underparts white with dark barring except on upper breast, which has irregular markings; uniform blackish hood and prominent broad blackish moustache; cheeks and throat pale; juveniles browner and with streaked underparts

● **HABITS**
Long periods of inactivity on nest or perched on cliff, pylon, tall building or in tree; soaring and dashing or diving hunting flights

● **VOICE**
A harsh, loud cackling *'rehk, rehk, rehk, rehk'* used in alarm; male's voice is higher pitched and less raucous than female's

● **FOOD**
Chiefly birds; hunting methods vary to suit prey species and terrain

● **BREEDING**
Mid-March to July; up to two weeks later in northern Britain; has a single brood but may lay replacement clutch if first one is lost

● **NEST**
Typically shallow scrape in soil or other debris on bare cliff ledge; also uses pylons or buildings; increasingly uses ledges on tall buildings

● **EGGS**
3–4 oval, buff or cream eggs with heavy reddish brown markings, laid at intervals of 2–3 days; incubation mainly by female for 28–33 days

● **YOUNG**
Female broods young for about 17 days while male hunts; fledge after 35–42 days; parents continue to provide food for two months

The top of the head is blackish and a prominent moustache can be seen on the cheek.

Distribution map key

■ Present all year round
□ Present during winter months

Blue-grey upperparts act as camouflage against rock faces.

The adults' underparts are mainly white, with dark barring on lower breast and belly.

The tail is rounded and the broad wings make it look relatively short.

PROTECTED!

The peregrine is afforded full protection at all times under the Wildlife and Countryside Act 1981, Schedule 1. Interference with the species or its nest is prohibited.

▲ Juvenile peregrines can be distinguished from adults by their browner plumage with brown streaks, not blackish bars, on buff underparts. Close-up views reveal that the base of the upper bill – the cere – is greyish blue, not yellow as in adults.

◄ The peregrine, although once endangered, is no longer on the critical list. In 2002 a survey by the British Trust for Ornithology revealed that Britain's peregrine population had increased by 10 per cent since 1991.

► Young peregrine chicks wait quietly in their precarious nest while the adults are away hunting. Peregrines raise one brood each year although replacement clutches are laid if the first clutch is lost.

The peregrine's habit of spending long periods perched on high rocks between hunting trips can make it a difficult bird to see. Its blue-grey back feathers serve as excellent camouflage, blending in particularly well with granite rock faces.

One way to improve the chances of a sighting is to locate a favourite resting perch – look for an accumulation of white droppings just below the perch. Another way is to search for plucking posts where the peregrines pluck and dismember their prey before eating it or carrying it to the nest. In this case the telltale sign will be feathers strewn beneath the post.

When looking for perches, bear in mind that the chosen resting point depends largely on the prevailing weather conditions. For example, on wet and windy days the birds are likely to choose sheltered places, while on calmer, warmer days they may visit more exposed sites.

Peregrines are territorial, and successful breeding depends on finding a suitable location with a sufficient supply of prey. Lowland peregrines normally remain on their breeding territories for the whole year. This is because the population is so high that if a pair leaves the area for any length of time, other birds may move in. Upland peregrines may be forced to leave their breeding grounds when food becomes scarce at the end of the summer. From August to early November many upland peregrines, especially females and juveniles, move to lowland or coastal sites where they remain for the winter months.

Choice of prey

The peregrine eats mainly birds. Its hunting preferences are reflected in its old names of duck hawk and pigeon hawk, but actually it has a much wider range of prey, from tiny goldcrests to herons and geese. Even tawny and little owls have been recorded as prey. The mainstay of its diet are medium-sized birds such as blackbirds, thrushes, starlings, pigeons and ducks.

Winter can be severe in the uplands. Many peregrines head for lowland or coastal areas in search of a better supply of food, although some birds, mainly adult males, remain. With less competition they manage to find enough prey to survive.

Display stoop

The speeding dive, or 'stoop' used by the peregrine while hunting is also an integral component of the bird's display flight, which it uses to attract a mate. Such aerial power and agility demonstrates a falcon's fitness to its chosen partner. These displays are mainly confined to within the nesting territory, usually close to the intended nest site.

Peregrines catch a high proportion of their prey in flight. When hunting, a bird either scans the area for prospective prey from an elevated vantage point or circles watchfully over its territory – a habit known by the old falconers' term of 'waiting on'.

When it spots a victim, the bird folds back its wings and drops into a wind-whistling dive known as a 'stoop'. At the last moment, the peregrine levels out and simply knocks the bird from the sky with a blow from its talons, instantly breaking its neck or back. Smaller birds may be plucked out of the air and in exceptional circumstances a peregrine may snatch a bird from the top of a tree or knock it from a rock ledge as it sweeps past.

Despite the peregrine's undeniable skill in the air, studies have shown that just a small percentage of stoops are successful, although some of the stoops recorded may have been practice dives or play.

Aerial mating displays

The peregrine puts its mastery of the air to another use when it wants to attract a mate and in spring there is a chance to see some spectacular pre-nesting displays. These include three types of display flight, each lasting for 10 to 20 minutes, which the peregrine performs at great speed.

The first of these is a spiralling display, in which a pair of peregrines circle each other as they attain great height. One bird then dives at the other in a mock stoop. The birds take turns at diving towards each other and occasionally the lower bird rolls over and presents its talons – the pair may even lock claws briefly. Despite appearances, such displays are not aggressive but demonstrate the bird's superb aerial ability and indicate an individual's fitness for breeding.

A second form of aerial display is known as the 'Z-flight', performed by a single peregrine, usually the male, and beginning with a high circling flight. The bird then flies level for some distance before flipping over on to its side and descending at speed. After another quick flip it levels off again. During a Z-flight, the pale underside and dark upperside become alternately visible, not only to the bird's mate but to any other peregrines nearby. In this way the performing

peregrine informs neighbouring birds that the territory is occupied as well as showing off its flying skills.

The third form of display is used by peregrines to establish or confirm their chosen nest site or eyrie. The bird takes off on rapidly vibrating wings and begins a horizontal figure-of-eight display. At times it almost brushes the rock face with its breast feathers, demonstrating its awesome agility. A slight miscalculation and the falcon could smash into the cliff.

Once the pair bond is established, the birds select a sheltered nesting site. This is typically a bare rock ledge on a cliff, with a slight depression scraped out in the dirt by the female using her chest and legs. Sometimes peregrines use old cliff nests of other species, such as ravens, although no new material is brought to the nest.

Birds of prey usually begin incubation as soon as the first egg is laid, but peregrines do not start incubation until

The stoop is entered from level flight. The wings are held still and drawn forward and the tail flexed down as the bird's forward momentum decreases.

The wings are then drawn back and held slightly away from the body, pitching the peregrine headlong into an almost vertical dive.

A twist of the tail and wings imparts a rotation to the dive.

The exit is very fast with wings and tail fully spread.

PLUNGE DIVE

To reach speeds of 250km/h (155mph) or more, the peregrine relies on gravity and power. A few swift wingbeats send it plunging earthwards from a high soaring flight. With its wings angled to form the shape of an arrowhead, gravity takes over.

Nevertheless, the peregrine's control of direction is superb. With the merest adjustment to the slant of its wing or a twist of its tail, the bird can change its angle and direction.

With its wings folded, the peregrine dives after its prey. It reaches an incredible speed and sometimes the force of the impact knocks the prey's head clean off its body.

PEREGRINE CALENDAR

JANUARY ● FEBRUARY

During the winter many peregrines inhabit coastal sites, preying on wildfowl and waders. However, some pairs remain at their lowland breeding areas to prevent maturing young from stealing their sites.

MARCH ● APRIL

In spring all the birds return to their breeding territories. Display flights may be seen as single birds look for mates. Eggs with heavy reddish brown markings are laid and hatch within days of each other.

MAY ● JUNE

The male provides food for his mate and young, while she broods and defends them. After the young fledge, they remain near the nest as they are still dependent on their parents for food.

JULY ● AUGUST

The adults teach the young how to hunt. As the young birds become proficient, resources within the home range become depleted – and they will be encouraged to seek out their own territory.

SEPTEMBER ● OCTOBER

By the autumn, the young should have left their home range, either voluntarily or driven away by their parents. They often head for the coast, where there is a reliable supply of food.

NOVEMBER ● DECEMBER

Some young peregrines inevitably starve in winter if they have not mastered the art of the speedy stoop. Adult birds complete their post-breeding moult and may move to the coast in search of food.

the last or penultimate egg has been laid. This has an advantage in that all the eggs hatch at around the same time, so all the hatchlings will be similar in size.

Providing for the young

Both the male and the female incubate the eggs, but just the female broods the newly hatched chicks. At this point the male becomes the sole provider for the family. On returning to the nest with prey he calls to his mate who leaves her chicks for a few moments to collect the food. The food may be placed on a nearby plucking post, where the male removes most the feathers to make the female's job of feeding the young easier. More spectacularly, the food may be passed from male to female on the wing. As the male flies in with the prey dangling from his talons, the female approaches him from below. At the last moment, the male drops the food and the female catches it by rolling over on to her back. She then returns to the nest to tear up the meat into pieces small enough to feed to her downy chicks. If the male supplies enough food, the young will survive. About two weeks after the young hatch, the female will also begin to hunt.

Adult peregrines are vigorous in the defence of their eggs and young. Some have even been known to attack rock climbers who have inadvertently ventured too close to an occupied ledge. The birds' loud, raucous calls are usually enough to deter most intruders.

When the chicks are five or six weeks old they leave the nest, but they remain dependent upon their parents for food for a further two months. During this time, they learn vital hunting skills by watching their parents. The adults train

The peregrine's fast and agile flight requires its plumage to be kept in tiptop condition. As part of its grooming routine, a peregrine takes a bath from time to time, as this one is doing in a mountain stream.

◀ The female tears up morsels of prey for her chicks until they are about four weeks old. Only in the last two weeks before fledging will the young be strong enough to manage this task by themselves.

their offspring by calling to them as they fly past with prey in their talons. Any chicks that are hungry enough take flight and pursue the parent until they can snatch or catch the prey. This training period is vitally important for the young birds because without the necessary flying and hunting skills, they will certainly perish with the onset of winter.

Conservation action

Peregrines have always suffered at the hands of egg collectors and poachers who steal chicks to sell on to Middle Eastern falconers. They are also persecuted by some gamekeepers and pigeon fanciers, even though they are protected by law. Yet in spite of these continued problems the biggest threat to peregrine survival over the past half century has been the use of organochlorine pesticides.

When these came into use in the mid 1950s to mid 1960s the peregrine went into a steep decline, as did many other bird species. The poisonous chemicals built up in the foodchain increasing the

▶ Although a blow from the peregrine's talons usually kills prey outright, larger birds, such as this red-legged partridge, might fall to the ground. The peregrine must then land to claim its prize.

death rate of adults and thinning the shells of their eggs. At the lowest point, in 1963, the peregrine population in Britain fell to fewer than 70 known pairs.

Fortunately, peregrine numbers started to make a steady comeback once the organochlorines were banned from sale. According to the RSPB, peregrines are now back to their pre-crash levels across much of their former range.

In fact, the bird is so numerous in some areas that breeding pairs have been sighted nesting on fairly insignificant 'gully' cliffs due to the lack of more appropriate sites. Some are even nesting in towns and cities, where ledges on churches and other high-rise buildings mimic their usual cliff sites. Today, the peregrine may be seen by a growing number of people – all of whom marvel at this powerful hunter of the skies.

In summer, peregrine falcons are found on moorland and other open areas where there are steep, rocky ledges for nest sites. An abundance of avian prey is also important for the peregrines to breed.

WILDLIFE WATCH

Where can I see peregrines?

● In spring and early summer peregrines can be seen across their full range. They hunt over moorland and open countryside and occasionally along woodland margins.

● In winter, hunting peregrines are regularly attracted to areas with large concentrations of wading birds or waterfowl. When these birds stop feeding and rise from the water calling in alarm, scan the skies for a hunting peregrine.

● By far the best place to see peregrines is at Symond's Yat overlooking the River Wye in Herefordshire. Forest Enterprise and the RSPB run a 'viewing programme' from 1 April to 31 August each year. High-powered telescopes are available to aid viewing of these spectacular birds. The best time to visit is in June when the parents are feeding their young. Telephone 01594 562852 for more details.

The crossbill

The colourful crossbill is a finch ideally adapted to life in a coniferous forest. Its bizarrely shaped bill is the perfect shape for prising open pine cones to reach the seeds inside.

The name of this finch fits it perfectly. Its crossed bill is a special adaptation that allows the bird to tweak open conifer cones and eat the seeds within. The lifestyle and habitat of the crossbill and its close relatives, the Scottish and parrot crossbills, are clearly dictated by their extraordinary specialist diet.

Conifer cones are normally a secure way for trees to protect their seeds before they ripen. The seeds are an important food source for many small mammals and birds, but one that is not available to most until the cones open naturally in spring, releasing the seeds. When this happens, the seeds are easily accessible to all that want them. With their specialised bills, however, crossbills can exploit the seeds

for many weeks before they become available to most other creatures. Squirrels, mice and great spotted woodpeckers can also break into pine cones. (The woodpecker uses its powerful bill to peck and prise a cone apart, having first wedged it in a crevice in a branch or tree stump. Squirrels and mice gnaw into the cones although mice usually have to wait until the cones fall to the ground, or are dropped by other creatures.)

Crossbills sometimes snip unripe cones off the twigs and then carry them to a convenient fork in a tree to feed on the seeds. However, they prefer to attack the cones when they are ripe and full of seeds, and even time their breeding to coincide with this.

The intensity of colour in the crossbill's plumage varies between individual birds and with the season. Males tend to appear darker and glossier later in the year as their feathers become worn.

DID YOU KNOW?

Just as humans can be left or right-handed, not all crossbills have mandibles (upper and lower parts of the bill) that cross the same way. Extensive surveys have revealed that just under half of all crossbills have upper mandibles that cross to the left, while the rest cross to the right. It seems unlikely that there is any advantage to being left or right-billed.

CROSSBILL FACT FILE

A large and acrobatic finch, the crossbill has variable plumage, which can be almost scarlet in males. The bill is heavy and crossed at the tip – a feature that occurs naturally only in this species and its close relatives.

● NAMES
Common names: crossbill, common crossbill
Scientific name: *Loxia curvirostra*

● HABITAT
Coniferous forests; also smaller stands of conifers, especially outside the breeding season

● DISTRIBUTION
Almost anywhere with mature, cone-bearing conifers, including Caledonian pine forests, Breckland in Norfolk and Kielder Forest in Northumberland

● STATUS
Number of resident and visiting birds fluctuates from a few thousand pairs to 20,000 pairs, with 100–500 pairs in Ireland, according to state of conifer cone crops

● SIZE
Length 16.5cm (6½in); weight 40g (1⅜oz)

● KEY FEATURES
Stocky with a large head and short forked tail; large, crossed bill. Adults streaky greyish brown with variable wash of colour. Males can be vivid red, salmon pink or orange with bright red rump; wings and tail dusky; females olive green with yellow rump; young males streaky pale grey-brown with patches of orange, red or yellow; young females sometimes dull green

● HABITS
Sociable, generally found in flocks

● VOICE
Flight call an explosive '*chip, chip, chip*'; rarely heard song is complex with warbles, trills and twitters

● FOOD
Conifer seeds, especially spruce and pine, also larch; sometimes seeds and other parts of other plants, and invertebrates

● BREEDING
Timing variable, for example, August–April in southern Scotland, December–June in eastern England with peak in February–April. One or two broods per year depending on conifer crop

● NEST
Conifer twigs, bark, lichen, moss and grass, lined with animal hair, moss and feathers; sited high in conifer tree

● EGGS
3–4 glossy, whitish, dark-spotted eggs; female incubates alone for 14–15 days

● YOUNG
Bill uncrossed at first; brooded for several days after hatching, fed by both parents; fledge after 20–25 days, parents continue to bring food for 3–6 weeks, probably until bill is fully crossed

Crossbills breed whenever there is a plentiful supply of pine seeds to feed the chicks. The parents masticate the seeds into an easily digestible mash before feeding them to their begging offspring.

Distribution map key

■ Present all year round

■ Occurs sporadically

PROTECTED!

All three species of crossbill receive full protection under the Wildlife and Countryside Act 1981, Schedule 1. It is illegal to interfere with the adult birds or to disturb their nests, eggs or young.

The stout bill has crossed mandibles.

The head is large and the neck thick.

Male plumage varies from vivid red to a dusky orange.

The tail is short with a distinct fork.

CROSSBILL CALENDAR

JANUARY • FEBRUARY

As the pine cones ripen, the breeding season is in full swing for crossbills in eastern England. The eggs are incubated for about 14 days and the young fledge three to four weeks later.

MARCH • APRIL

At first the young birds have uncrossed bills. They continue to be fed by their parents until their crossed mandibles develop six weeks or so later. Then they are able to feed easily on open cones.

MAY • JUNE

As the population is boosted by newly fledged young, crossbills leave their home forests. Having depleted the year's conifer crop, they must find new areas where the cones will be plentiful next year.

JULY • AUGUST

Crossbills continue to roam in search of food. This is a good time of year to spot these birds, as they come to drink at forest puddles. In Scotland, the crossbills are just entering the breeding season.

SEPTEMBER • OCTOBER

Most crossbills have now settled into the areas where they will breed later in the year. Conifers are beginning to form cones and the birds are less likely to be seen away from the treetops.

NOVEMBER • DECEMBER

Even though snow may cover the ground, crossbills living in eastern England begin to breed. Nest building and even egg laying will already be taking place in some places despite the freezing weather.

The number of conifer seeds taken by crossbills is huge. It has been calculated that one brood of crossbills can consume 90,000 spruce seeds while in the nest. Not surprisingly, the distribution of crossbills is closely related to the incidence of conifer forests.

Once crossbills have selected a mate, the pair bond lasts for just one season. It takes the work of both female (left) and male to ensure that the young receive enough food to survive and thrive.

Detailed observations of breeding females emphasise how important it is for them to supplement their diet of conifer seeds with additional mineral-rich foods, including male conifer flowers and buds and invertebrates. These provide the essential nutrients that the female birds need for egg formation. Obtaining enough calcium to form the eggshell is often a problem. Some may be derived from the hard skeletons of invertebrates, such as woodlice and millipedes. If necessary, crossbills have been known to

supplement their diets with apples and other fruit, or with mortar, putty and even slivers of bone, when they can find it.

Crossbills are stimulated to breed by an abundance of food, whenever it may occur. Birds in southern Scotland build their nests in spruce trees and lay their eggs between August and April, while those that depend upon pine cones in eastern England lay their eggs from December to June, with a peak from February to April. Crossbills in Ireland usually lay their eggs one month later.

Arboreal acrobats

Crossbills are skilled at extracting seeds from within the closed scales of conifer cones, often while the cones are still attached to the tree. Despite their plump appearance, the birds are agile when feeding. They frequently hang upside down in much the same manner as much smaller and lighter tits.

Crossbills have strong feet and legs, as they need to be extremely acrobatic when attacking cones on the trees.

The bill is sometimes used, parrot fashion, to grip a branch while the crossbill manoeuvres itself into position.

The bird holds the cone against the underside of the branch with one or both feet to prevent it from moving around as it picks out the seeds.

At first the chicks have straight bills, but their mandibles start to cross a couple of weeks after hatching and are fully crossed about six weeks after the birds have left the nest.

Mobile feeder

Crossbills are not routine migrants, but they are very mobile within their territories because their food supply is seldom consistently good in exactly the same locality in successive years. In many parts of their wide northern and eastern European breeding range, where much of the land is covered with conifers, there is usually no need for the birds to move far – the next woodland or clump of hills will often support an adequate crop if their home patch fails.

However, the birds can face problems in places where they feed only on spruce because these trees produce good crops of cones just once every few years. As a result, some crossbill populations are nomadic, the birds moving to locations outside their usual territories in search of food each year.

In the good years, all of the spruce trees over a wide area may bear a bumper crop. This enables hundreds of thousands of crossbill pairs to breed very productively.

PARROT CROSSBILL

A relative of the crossbill and the Scottish crossbill, the parrot crossbill, *Loxia pytyopsittacus,* can sometimes be seen in British conifer forests. These birds usually breed farther to the east, in Eurasia, where they can be found living in pine forests. Although sedentary by nature, when the pine seed crop fails they are forced to move in search of food and sizeable flocks have been known to spread as far as Scotland and the east coast of England. Parrot crossbills sometimes breed in Britain, generally in the same locations as the Scottish crossbill, although very occasionally in East Anglia.

Parrot crossbills are difficult to distinguish from their native cousins. They are very similar in colour but generally look bulkier with an even heavier, deeper bill and a thicker neck.

A crossbill will flutter easily from twig to twig, then sidle along a branch and hang from a cone while it feeds. Its legs and toes are adapted for grasping the cones and keeping them steady.

In this case, the huge numbers of youngsters that result may force a large proportion of the population to relocate and make journeys that cover thousands of miles.

It may have been just this kind of scenario in the crossbill's European breeding grounds that led to the birds' arrival in Britain. A crossbill invasion occurred in the 13th century and another in Tudor times. According to one record, great alarm was caused as they settled on the apple orchards of Kent and shredded the fruit to get at the seeds.

Erratic arrivals

All over Europe crossbills are ringed for research purposes and records show that, in some years, the crossbills reaching Britain have originated in Scandinavia. In other years, the birds come from farther to the east, when they may include a rare

visitor, the two-barred crossbill. These mass movements, known as 'irruptions', may occur several times in a decade or not at all. Some immigrants eventually return to their country of origin, maybe after just one season or not until after they have established new populations.

The expansion of conifer forests in Britain in the 20th century has led to increased breeding opportunities for crossbills because, unlike many other bird species, they will breed in their adopted land if they find suitable food. During a recent migration to Breckland in Norfolk, crossbills were the most conspicuous bird to be seen over vast tracts of woodland for several months. In the huge Kielder Forest in Northumbria, counts following an irruption in November and December 1990 indicated there may have been as many as 40,000 crossbills in the forest.

Research into the DNA of crossbills suggests that there may turn out to be 15 or even 20 different species. This would present a real problem for birdwatchers, who find it hard enough already to distinguish between the three species regularly found in Britain.

Cone raider

The crossbill's remarkable beak is essential when it comes to feeding on pine seeds, which are protected by tightly sealed cones.

The crossbill inserts the tips of its mandibles between the scales of the cone. It then moves the lower mandible sideways, forcing the scale open.

The birds have extremely strong neck muscles to exert the necessary force to prise open the scales of unripe cones.

With the scales parted from the cone, the crossbill simply scoops out the seed with its long, strong tongue.

SUPERBLY ADAPTED BILLS

The size of the crossbill's beak varies between the three species regularly found in Britain and is related to the toughness of the cones that are favoured by the different birds. The crossbill (below left)

prefers to feed on the soft cones produced by the spruce tree, and has the smallest bill. The scales of these cones are easier to prise apart than those of the pine tree. The bill of the Scottish crossbill

(centre) is next in size, while the parrot crossbill (right) has the largest bill of all of them. Both Scottish and parrot crossbills use their bills to extract and eat the seeds from pine cones.

The crossbill has a smaller head and bill than the other two species. Its mandibles are sharply pointed, very curved and fully crossed at the tips to access spruce seeds.

The Scottish crossbill's head is larger than that of the crossbill, and its bill is deeper and blunter. This adaptation enables the bird to extract seeds from pine cones.

The parrot crossbill has a thick neck and striking parrot-like bill. Its mandibles are less crossed than those of the crossbill. This species favours tougher pine cones.

WILDLIFE WATCH

Where can I see crossbills?

● Mature conifer plantations are the best places to look, once the trees start to produce cones and the forests have become dense, dark thickets. Crossbills are among the relatively few birds that thrive there.

● Crossbills are often noisy while flying around. As they feed, they utter a soft, clipped call that is rendered *'chip, chip'* – the first sign that they are present. Other clues are the discarded cones scattered all over the ground. If cones are heard or seen falling to the ground, crossbills are feeding overhead.

● Fortunate birdwatchers may encounter a singing crossbill perched at the top of a tree, uttering a loud and pleasant mixture of chirps and warbles. These often include nasal notes, rather like those of a redpoll.

● From late May to autumn, crossbills are on the move and may be seen flying overhead anywhere in the country. Listen out for their distinctive flight call, a harder, more explosive version of the feeding call – they are likely to be heard before they are seen. Since crossbills must traverse areas without conifers in their search for new breeding sites, they may be seen foraging for weed seeds from plants on the ground, as well as taking fruit and seeds from trees.

SCOTTISH CROSSBILL

Once considered to be a subspecies of crossbill, the Scottish crossbill was given separate species status about 25 years ago. This makes it Britain's only endemic bird – that is, a species found nowhere else in the world.

Scottish crossbills were once thought to be hybrids between the crossbill and the parrot crossbill. They are certainly midway in size between the other two, and at a distance they can be easily mistaken for a large-billed crossbill or a small-billed parrot crossbill. The three species cannot even be distinguished on the basis of distribution, as in some years they all breed in the same area.

The fate of the Scottish crossbill is inextricably linked to that of the remaining mature Scots pine forests in the ancient Caledonian forests of northern Scotland. They often breed in the same or adjacent woods in successive years. They can usually find at least some trees bearing cones, scouring the area and investigating the remotest Scots pines for food. Once the crossbills locate a decent crop of cones, the tree will be visited regularly until there are no suitable cones left.

In February the Scottish crossbill builds a platform of twigs, high in the fork of an old pine tree. Its breeding is synchronised with the ripening of Scots pine cones so that its young can feed themselves before the seed harvest is exhausted.

The Scottish crossbill has found a sanctuary in the remains of the ancient Caledonian pine forests of Scotland. It moves through the canopy in groups, often uttering its distinctive *'chip, chip'* calls from high up on the tips of the branches.

The common lizard

A range of locations can support common lizards, provided there are enough suitable sunny spots for basking. If the sun gets too hot, they will quickly retreat to the shade of a rocky crevice.

Found all over mainland Britain as well as the Isle of Man, the Isle of Wight, Anglesey and several of the Inner Hebridean islands, the common lizard is the only reptile to occur naturally in Ireland. It lives in mountainous regions, at altitudes as high as 1000m (3300ft), and also favours heathland, sand dunes, woodland, hedgerows and railway embankments, whether dry or damp.

The common lizard has suffered less from changes to the countryside caused by humans than other reptiles. In some places, it has even increased its range, colonising overgrown dune systems where the water table has dropped. However, the animals are susceptible to intensive farming activities and the loss of heath-land to agriculture, forestry and housing has had a serious effect on numbers.

Adaptable reptile

Like all lizards, the common lizard enjoys lying in the sun but it is also one of the most cold-tolerant of all the world's reptiles, which is why it survives in a climate that is not reliably sunny. Its optimum body temperature is 30°C (86°F), which can usually be reached in summer by basking. They emerge from their night's sleep in a safe refuge with a body temperature of about 15°C (59°F). Once they have warmed up sufficiently, they can spend time hunting.

Lizards have several techniques they can employ for increasing heat absorption. One is to flatten the body to increase the area exposed to the sun. A lizard may also tilt itself upwards, stretch its legs and, at times, turn up the soles of its feet to warm them too.

PARASITES

Lizards are susceptible to attack from a variety of parasites, which live and feed on the living animal but do not kill it. The most obvious are bloodsucking mites and ticks. These can sometimes be seen on a common lizard's skin or hiding under its scales. Mites can transmit fatal infections while sucking their host's blood. The sheep tick is, perhaps surprisingly, a parasite of the species, secreting itself behind the common lizard's foreleg. The tick is especially prevalent in the New Forest.

Other parasites live inside the lizard's gut, including at least one species of tapeworm and one of the nematode worms. In an infected animal, they share the available space with a multitude of single-celled organisms, none of which appear to do any major damage to their host.

A rustle in the undergrowth or the sight of a small tail disappearing into the grass are usually the only signs that a common lizard is present. This nimble reptile disappears in a flash when disturbed.

COMMON LIZARD FACT FILE

An adaptable creature, the common lizard forms loose colonies in a variety of habitats, and is the only reptile found in Scotland and Ireland. It has a slender body, a small, rounded head and its tail is twice as long as its body.

Distribution map key

■	Present
□	Not present

● **NAMES**
Common names: common lizard, viviparous lizard
Scientific name: *Lacerta vivipara*

● **HABITAT**
Very varied; rocky upland, heaths, hedgerows, woodlands, sand dunes, grassy banks and waste ground

● **DISTRIBUTION**
Widespread though patchy throughout the British Isles

● **STATUS**
Steady decline in recent years; about 1,200,000 breeding adults

● **SIZE**
Total length typically 13–15cm (5–6in)

● **KEY FEATURES**
Dull brownish colour, occasionally grey, dark green, reddish or black; males darker than females; dark stripe extends from back of head to base of tail; flanks dark; rows of white or pale yellow spots on back and flanks; male's belly bright yellow, orange or sometimes red with dense black spots; female's belly usually yellowish-white or grey with few or no spots

● **HABITS**
Hibernates in groups of 12 or more individuals from mid to late October to mid to late February; males emerge first, followed by juveniles, then females

The common lizard is protected against deliberate killing, injury or collection for sale under the Wildlife and Countryside Act, Schedule 5.

● **VOICE**
Mostly silent; may hiss when fighting

● **FOOD**
Insects and larvae, spiders, earthworms and other invertebrates; drinks rain, dew and aphid honeydew

● **BREEDING**
Mates in April or May; 3–11 live young born in membrane late June to September (mainly July)

● **NEST**
Secluded, damp hollow for giving birth; hibernation dens in holes and crevices and between tree roots

● **YOUNG**
37–44mm (1½–1¾in) at birth; black, dark brown or bronze above and dirty white below; adult pattern develops quickly; tail much shorter than in adult

● **SIGNS**
Sloughed (cast-off) skins

Five dark stripes, sometimes broken into spots, run from the back of the head to the base of the tail.

Rows of pale yellowish or whitish spots occur alongside dark markings.

In males, the tail comprises two-thirds of the total body length; it is slightly shorter in females.

During prolonged hot spells, common lizards often prove difficult to find because they retreat under cover. Not only may the weather be too hot, but by staying out in the open when it is very dry lizards risk dehydration. At such times, they enter a short period of summer hibernation – known as 'aestivation' – usually in a burrow or crevice.

Common lizards use similar sites for winter hibernation from mid-October onwards, but are easily tempted out by mild weather. They may even venture out with snow on the ground. At such times, lizards have been seen to emerge from their burrows dragging their hindquarters behind them, as if partly frozen or paralysed. Their back legs soon recover after a couple of minutes in the sun.

Reptiles cannot maintain their body temperature in the same way as mammals and are referred to as cold-blooded, or ectothermic. By hibernating during the coldest months, lizards avoid freezing to death and conserve energy by remaining inactive at a time when their insect prey is scarce.

Hazardous existence
Like most small animals, common lizards represent convenient food for numerous predators. They feature in the diets of adders and especially smooth snakes

The female common lizard gives birth to her whole brood either at the same time or over a period of one or two days. The young are born fully formed, each encased in a transparent membrane.

▼ The common lizard keeps its body temperature stable by basking in the sun and cooling down in the shade. In weak sunshine, the animal flattens its body to increase the area exposed to the warmth.

► Common lizards often take to water to catch food such as insects that have become trapped in the surface film. Lizards are good swimmers and can also stay underwater for several minutes.

as well as a host of birds, from blackbirds to buzzards. They are also preyed upon by rats, hedgehogs, foxes, badgers and weasels. Domestic cats have reduced the common lizard populations of gardens and railway embankments. Young lizards, which are no more than 44mm (1¾in) long at birth, may be eaten by shrews, toads, robins and even large beetles.

Due to its small size, the common lizard often has to rely upon speed to escape predators. If startled, it may take to water. It can swim well and can also dive to the bottom of fast-flowing streams to hide among submerged rocks. Common lizards have been known to remain underwater for up to nine minutes.

Lizards suffer high juvenile mortality and the life expectancy of a newborn common lizard is less than a year. There is greater mortality among females than males and only one in ten common lizards reaches the age of 13 years.

Avoiding capture

All three species of lizard found in Britain (the common lizard, sand lizard and slow-worm) can lose all or part of their tails as a means of defence. If a predator is left with the tail, it may focus on that rather than the escaping lizard. Shedding, or autotomy, is usually a response to the tail being seized. Fracture points in the bones of the vertebral column enable the tail to snap and the lizard to leave it behind.

The attentions of an inquisitive puppy alarm this common lizard. Hoping to divert the puppy's attention while it scuttles to safety, the lizard prepares to shed its tail.

When the tail is about to be shed, the eight muscles that surround the lizard's tail bone contract, losing contact with the muscles behind, thus assisting the fracture of the tail.

Fast breeding
Mating takes place in April or May. Each male common lizard defends a poorly defined territory against other males. Any female that wanders into the territory is pursued along the resident male's regular feeding trails, sometimes for several hours. The chase eventually draws to a close and the male sits in front of the female, vibrating his tail. Suddenly, he

The lost tail convulses wildly for several minutes after it is shed, which startles and distracts the puppy. There is little bleeding and the lizard's tail stump soon heals.

▲ Young common lizards are usually much darker than their parents and do not acquire the striking patterns of the adults until the following year. Their colour helps them to avoid the attention of predators.

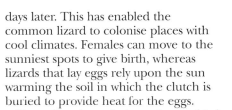

seizes her in his jaws by the head or flanks and they mate. While they are immobile, the lizards are vulnerable to predators and so mating is swift, lasting only a few minutes – at most it may occur on and off for up to 35 minutes.

In early summer, pregnant females spend a lot of time basking to encourage their eggs to develop inside them. They drink frequently but hardly feed at all, living off fat stored during the previous autumn. Pregnancy lasts three months and by the end of this period the eggs may comprise 40 per cent of the mother's body weight. She gives birth in a secluded, shaded and usually damp hollow.

Breaking free

The common lizard is often referred to as 'viviparous', which means 'giving birth to live young'. Like the slow-worm, smooth snake and adder, it gives birth to well-developed young rather than producing eggs. The young are born encased in a transparent membrane, which may be broken at birth, or up to two or three days later. This has enabled the common lizard to colonise places with cool climates. Females can move to the sunniest spots to give birth, whereas lizards that lay eggs rely upon the sun warming the soil in which the clutch is buried to provide heat for the eggs.

Young lizards are independent at birth. As soon as they shed the membrane, they chase prey and feed just like adults. They grow rapidly, sloughing their skins three times before hibernation, by which time they have doubled in length. The young are often active later than adults because they are able to warm up adequately even in weak sunshine. Male lizards are sexually mature by their second year, but females have to wait a further year before they can breed.

▲ The biggest broods comprise 11 babies and are usually produced by the largest females. The young are born in midsummer and receive no care from their mother.

WILDLIFE WATCH

Where can I see common lizards?

● Open, sunny places, such as grassy, south-facing banks, are favoured by common lizards. They bask on rocks or logs and, because they are good climbers, can often be found in the cracks and crevices of old walls.

● Look for them first thing in the morning or in the late afternoon when they will be less active.

● In cooler weather, look under pieces of wood for sloughed skins and even resting lizards.

● Lizards will disappear at the slightest hint of movement, sound or shadow, so use binoculars to pick out likely basking sites. When approaching, make sure that no shadows fall on the area to be searched – and be patient.

Growing a replacement tail can take several years, so common lizards with just a stump are not unusual. Occasionally, individuals with two or even three tails may be seen, because more than one new tail can develop from the fracture point.

Recognising upland butterflies

Green-veined whites and meadow browns may sometimes be seen in surprising profusion, as well as the mountain ringlet – Britain's one true alpine butterfly.

The problems associated with the generally harsh environment of the uplands mean that just a few species of butterfly can survive there. Nevertheless, butterflies and day-flying moths are often the most conspicuous insects to be found in these regions and they can sometimes occur in large numbers.

Members of the main butterfly families are represented, including the handsome, acrobatic fritillaries, the more subtly marked browns, the fragile-looking whites and the diminutive blues.

One of the more abundant species is the meadow brown, which is common on unfertilised grassland throughout Britain, including upland regions. In high summer you may see clouds of meadow brown butterflies rise out of patches of long grass. On hazy days they may rest with their brown wings outspread, displaying the characteristic orange patch and single eyespot on the forewings.

The green-veined white is another common species. It thrives in a range of damp places, including the edges of woodland in upland regions and on grassy moorland. As its name suggests, its wings are marked with greyish green scales along the veins and these are especially prominent on the underside.

Limestone pavements and sheltered cliffs are good places to look out for the low-flying northern brown argus. Despite its name, this is classified as a blue butterfly. It may be seen resting or feeding on rock rose, the main food plant for its caterpillars.

Food plants

One prerequisite for all butterflies – and a useful clue to finding them – is the presence of food plants for their caterpillars. Where mat-grass and sheep's fescue grow, mountain ringlets may be found, while the Scotch argus seeks blue moor-grass in the north of England and purple moor-grass in Scotland.

Male green-veined white butterflies shower females with a lemon scent strong enough to be detectable by humans.

EASY GUIDE TO SPOTTING UPLAND BUTTERFLIES

WHAT ARE UPLAND BUTTERFLIES?

● The mountain ringlet and Scotch argus belong to a subgroup of the family Nymphalidae known as browns. All the British brown butterflies have eyespots on their wings, which are thought to draw attacks by birds away from the insect's body. By late summer, eyespots often bear the scars of such encounters.

● Of the nine species of true fritillaries that occur in Britain, all of which belong to another subgroup of the family Nymphalidae, two are found in upland regions. These are the high brown and the dark green fritillary. Both sexes have small, brush-like forelegs and are powerful fliers.

● The green-veined white belongs to the white family Pieridae. It has broad, rounded hind wings and angled forewings. Unlike its relative, the cabbage white, it is not a garden pest because its caterpillars feed on wild cruciferous plants. Its flight is weak and fluttering.

● The northern brown argus is a member of the family Lycaenidae, commonly known as blue butterflies. The upperwing markings are almost identical in both sexes.

Distribution map key

[ ] Present   [ ] Not present

Mating pairs of butterflies, such as these meadow browns, often remain in tandem for up to an hour.

NORTHERN BROWN ARGUS *Aricia artaxerxes*

Scottish populations of this butterfly have a white spot on the forewing, which is not seen on those found in northern England. Not a gregarious species, males tend to drive away rivals. One brood a year is usual.

● SIZE
Wingspan about 30mm (1¼in)

● FOODPLANT FOR LARVAE
Mainly common rock rose

● CHRYSALIS
In low vegetation

● ADULT SEASON
June–September

● HABITAT
Grassy slopes

● DISTRIBUTION
Scattered localities in northern England and Scotland

The northern brown argus prefers sheltered, well-drained, limestone hillsides and seldom strays from its known haunts.

Forewings have a distinctive white spot (typically Scottish colonies only)

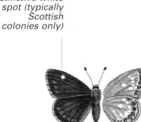

Upperwings brown with orange crescents or spots

Underwings grey brown with white-bordered black spots

SCOTCH ARGUS *Erebia aethiops*

As its name suggests, the Scotch argus is most common north of the border. It resembles the mountain ringlet but is smaller and has white centres to black eyespots on its upperwings. It is so dependent on sunshine to keep it warm that it will stop flying if a cloud passes in front of the sun.

● SIZE
Wingspan about 48mm (2in)

● FOODPLANT FOR LARVAE
Purple and blue moor-grass

● CHRYSALIS
Hidden low down in dense grass or moss

● ADULT SEASON
July–August

● HABITAT
Damp grassland up to 500m (1640ft), edges of bogs and woodland clearings

● DISTRIBUTION
Northern England and Scotland

The Scotch argus prefers to rest on vegetation with its wings spread out flat. Being relatively sluggish, it is usually easy to observe.

Upperwings dark chocolate brown with orange bands and white centres to its black eyespots

Underside of forewing has pattern similar to that on upperwing

Underside of hind wing is marbled greyish brown

MOUNTAIN RINGLET *Erebia epiphron*

This is one of just a handful of British butterflies that are confined to northern upland regions rather than straying to the lowland south. It is active on sunny days only, disappearing into cover as soon as the sun goes in. When the sun reappears, it sunbathes for brief periods with its brown wings outstretched.

● **SIZE**
Wingspan about 33mm(1¼in)

● **FOODPLANT FOR LARVAE**
Mat-grass

● **CHRYSALIS**
In loose cocoon of silk and grass at base of food plant

● **ADULT SEASON**
Late June–July

● **HABITAT**
Grassy moorland

● **DISTRIBUTION**
Lake District up to 700m (2300ft) and up to 1000m (3300ft) in parts of western Scottish Highlands

The mountain ringlet remains in its upland habitat whatever the weather and its wings can soon begin to look ragged.

Upperwings chocolate brown

Underwing pattern similar to that on upperwing, but colours are duller

Orange bands on forewings and hind wings have dark spots

HIGH BROWN FRITILLARY *Argynnis adippe*

A strong-flying and attractive butterfly, the high brown fritillary has broad, fairly rounded wings. The upperwings are a rich orange brown, marked with well-defined black spots and lines. The underwings are buffish brown with green scaling on the hind wings. The hind wings also have a row of reddish eyespots.

● **SIZE**
Wingspan about 65mm (2½in)

● **FOODPLANT FOR LARVAE**
Usually common dog violet

● **CHRYSALIS**
Brownish-black and spiny; resembles a dead leaf; suspended from leaf stalk

● **ADULT SEASON**
Late June–mid-August

● **HABITAT**
High, open areas, including moors, meadows and woodland margins

● **DISTRIBUTION**
Confined to western and north-western England

On sunny days, high brown fritillaries are on the wing, not coming to rest until the late afternoon.

Forewings less rounded at the tip than dark green fritillary

Underwing markings reflect those on upper surface

Ground colour of upperwings orange brown

Distinctive red-ringed spots on hind wings

DARK GREEN FRITILLARY *Argynnis aglaja*

A large butterfly, very similar to the high brown, the dark green fritillary is beautifully marked with more rounded forewings. The underside of the hind wings has greenish scaling and silvery spots. The dark green fritillary prefers open ground. It takes nectar from thistles and often rests on the ground or on bracken.

● **SIZE**
Wingspan about 60mm (2⅜in)

● **FOODPLANT FOR LARVAE**
Usually common dog-violet

● **CHRYSALIS**
Reddish brown with black markings; resembles dead leaf; suspended from leaf stalk

● **ADULT SEASON**
July–August

● **HABITAT**
Chalk downs, moors and sand dunes

● **DISTRIBUTION**
Widespread but very local

When the dark green fritillary is seen resting with its wings folded, the extensive greenish hue of the underside of the hind wing is noticeable.

Wing less angled at tip than high brown fritillary

Underwings buffish-brown to orange brown

Ground colour of upperwings orange brown

Conspicuous silvery spots on underside of hind wing; no red eyespots

Upland orchids

Many of these plants are small with greenish flowers, but like all orchids, they possess a delicate beauty that makes finding them well worth the effort.

Orchids are arguably the most sought-after of all wild flowers and plenty are to be found in upland regions. For some, such as the lesser twayblade, the higher ground provides the precise conditions they need, while for other more adaptable species, such as the common twayblade, the uplands are just one of many places in which they can thrive.

Often it is the habitat in which they grow that helps to distinguish between closely related species. For example, the heath spotted-orchid, which flourishes on moors and acidic heathland, is closely related to the common

spotted-orchid that inhabits the chalky soils of lowland England. The flowers and leaves may look similar, but if the plant is growing on acidic moorland, it is likely to be a heath spotted-orchid.

Specialised orchids

One unusual species found growing in moist, mossy or peaty areas of pine or birch woods in Scotland and northern England is the coralroot orchid. This plant has very little chlorophyll (the pigment used by plants to convert light energy into food) and, as a result, it has to obtain nutrients in some other way. Along with two

non-upland species – the bird's nest orchid and the rare ghost orchid – the coralroot is classed as a 'saprophyte'. This means that it feeds indirectly via fungi growing within its roots. In the coralroot orchid, the roots form a creamy coloured mass of rounded knobs resembling coral, hence its name. The fungi living inside them produce valuable nutrients from decaying matter in the soil. Strictly speaking, the coralroot orchid is not a true saprophyte because some cells in its flowering stems usually contain a small amount of chlorophyll.

Pollination of coralroot orchids is generally carried out by small flies or beetles, although some self-pollination takes place, too.

Other upland orchids include the lesser butterfly orchid, found on moors and bogs, the fragrant orchid, which is seen on hilly grassland, and the Lapland marsh orchid, discovered in 1986 growing in hilly, damp areas in north-west Scotland.

The distinctive mauve-pink colouring of the heath spotted-orchid is particularly attractive to bees, which pollinate the tall spikes of flowers.

UPLAND ORCHID FACT FILE

● Heath spotted-orchid
Dactylorhiza maculata
Habitat and distribution
Common on acidic moorland and heath; relatively uncommon in lowland England, but widespread in north and west Ireland, and whole of north and west Britain
Size Up to 25cm (10in)
Key features
Leaves narrow, pointed, usually with circular purplish spots; flowers arranged in dense, blunt spikes, usually pinkish with purple streaks and spots, and have broad, flat unlobed lower lip with a small central tooth
Flowering time
Mid-June–late July

● Lesser twayblade
Listera cordata
Habitat and distribution
Damp acidic woodland and moorland in north and west of British Isles but absent from much of lowland England
Size 4–10cm (1½–4in), but usually only about 5cm (2in)
Key features
Distinctive single pair of heart-shaped leaves; flowers (3–15) usually dull reddish green; flowering very irregular, detecting non-flowering plants is difficult
Flowering time
June–August

● Bog orchid
Hammarbya paludosa
Habitat and distribution
Wet, acidic areas, often in *Sphagnum* moss; widespread in the north and west of the British Isles, but rare or extinct in much of lowland England (except in New Forest bogs); erratic growth – may be rare one year and quite common the next
Size 3–8cm (1¼–3in)
Key features
Smallest, most inconspicuous British orchid; up to 4 small ovate leaves on the lower part of the stem; tiny bulbils (bulblike reproductive organs) that form on leaf-edges fall off to form new plants; flower tiny, yellowish green, lip – 2mm (½in) long and unspurred – uppermost, a position achieved by 360 degree twist in flower stalk (in most orchids, lip lowermost because flower stalk turns through 180 degrees in development)
Flowering time
July–September

● Frog orchid
Dactylorhiza viridis
Habitat and distribution
Widespread in British Isles, but commonest in Scotland where it grows on upland, mountain ledges and in a variety of grassland habitats
Size 5–20cm (2–8in), but usually no more than 15cm (6in)
Key features
Small, low-growing; numerous small, yellowish green flowers often more or less suffused with reddish brown, supposed to resemble a jumping frog; outer flower segments form hood over green strap-shaped, three-lobed lip, middle lobe folded back; variable in size and number of flowers; faint, sweet scent
Flowering time
June–August

● Coralroot orchid
Corallorhiza trifida
Habitat and distribution
A northern orchid, commonest in mossy woods of mixed pine and birch in Scotland, and extending southwards to Yorkshire; absent from both Wales and Ireland
Size 10–20cm (4–8in)
Key features
Yellowish stems in small clumps with 2–4 long, sheathing leaves; 4–12 slightly drooping flowers, yellowish or brownish green with a white lip; roots thick and rounded, resembling coral
Flowering time
June–July

WILDLIFE WATCH

Where can I find upland orchids?

● The frog orchid is widespread in Scotland, especially in the mountains and near the sea.

● The coralroot orchid is a plant of pine and birchwoods and scrubby dune slacks in Scotland.

● The best places to search for the bog orchid are the uplands of Wales, far northern England and Scotland. It also occurs in some New Forest bogs.

● Look for the lesser twayblade in the north-west of Britain and Ireland.

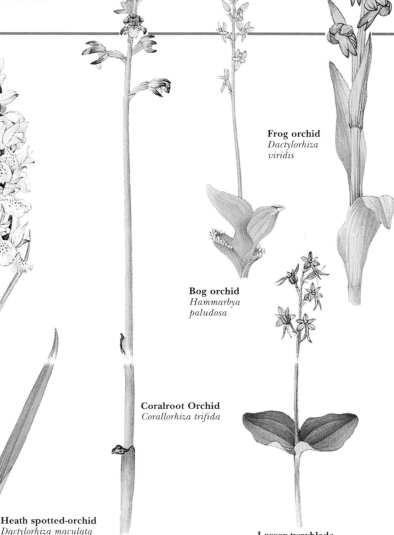

Frog orchid
Dactylorhiza viridis

Bog orchid
Hammarbya paludosa

Coralroot Orchid
Corallorhiza trifida

Heath spotted-orchid
Dactylorhiza maculata

Lesser twayblade
Listera cordata

The frog orchid occurs in most of the British Isles but its small size and yellowish green flowers make it difficult to spot.

Insect-eating plants

In soil where vital nutrients are limited, some plants have
evolved remarkable strategies to lure and capture insects
in order to feed on their bodies.

In some hostile habitats, the soils are so impoverished that plants have difficulty extracting enough nutrients to survive. Some species, however, have evolved techniques that enable them to supplement their diet with food from another source. Insects are lured, entrapped and then digested at leisure. The best-known insectivorous plant, the Venus fly trap, comes from North America, as do the pitcher plants, but there are a number of British insect-eating species. Each has its own method of attracting and snaring the unwary.

Sundews have leaves covered with tiny hairs, each of which carries a glistening bead that looks just like a droplet of water, even on the warmest summer days (hence the name 'sundew'). Thirsty insects, attracted to the illusion of water, discover too late that it is in fact a glue-like secretion capable of sticking any insect firmly to the leaf surface. The leaf is astonishingly sensitive – as the insect struggles, it touches other hairs, which react to the stimulus by bending towards the creature, helping to ensnare it further.

Sensory bristles surrounding
the trapdoors on bladderwort
plants detect the passing of tiny
aquatic insects, such as this
water flea, and spring the trap.

Once caught, there is no escape from the trap. If the insect is large, the whole leaf folds over, smothering it. Digestive juices are secreted to break down the soft parts of the insect's body and valuable nutrients are absorbed.

Amazingly, the plant is able to differentiate between the touch of possible prey and false alarms, such as falling raindrops or movement by wind. Continued pressure must be exerted on an extremely small portion of the leaf to initiate a response.

Other plant traps

Bladderworts are aquatic plants with long, floating, branched stems bearing submerged, feathery leaves. Each leaf is deeply divided into threadlike segments clothed with minute bristles. Some or all of the stems bear tiny transparent sacs, or bladders. Each bladder contains a gland that absorbs some of the water in the

bladder, thereby creating a vacuum. When a small aquatic animal, such as a water flea, brushes past the bladder, a trapdoor springs open and the creature is sucked inside. The remaining water swirls around, pushing the door shut and trapping the prey. Once the animal has been digested, the trap is reset. This mechanism is so successful that the plant does not need roots to gather nutrients.

The butterwort – so named because an extract from the leaves causes milk to curdle – is less dependent on insects for food. To the human touch, the rosette of broad yellow-green leaves feels slightly tacky, but to a small insect the leaves are inescapably sticky. Once an insect is trapped, digestive juices are secreted from glands on the surface of the leaf.

A blue damselfly is caught by
the long-stalked glands around
the edge of sundew leaves. The
insect's body is broken down by
protein-digesting enzymes
secreted by the leaves.

WILDLIFE WATCH

Where can I see insectivorous plants?

● Sundews can be found growing in damp, acidic places around pool margins.

● Bladderworts are fully aquatic, growing in bog pools.

● Butterworts grow in boggy patches and around standing pools on hills and mountains.

● Pitcher plants, much larger and more spectacular than many native British insect-eating plants, are occasionally found on damp upland and heathland. They are well established in bogs in central Ireland and also grow in parts of southern England and the Lake District.

Pitcher plants have remarkable leaves that are folded and joined to make a tubular water trap, or 'pitcher'. Flies are attracted to sweet nectar secreted from the top leaf, or 'hood', which partially covers the pitcher. As a fly investigates, it is encouraged by yet more nectar to go down inside the leaf tube, which is usually half filled with a mixture of rainwater, dew and a digestive enzyme. Close to the water-level, a band of downward-facing hairs causes the insect to lose its footing and it topples into a watery grave. In a good season, the plant may fill up with undigestible body parts, so it needs to replace the pitchers annually.

The plants still need to be pollinated and while some insects are being digested at the base of the plant, others are being rewarded for their services. The nectar-producing flowers are positioned well above the foliage so that the helpful insects, such as bees, are unlikely to be ensnared and eaten.

INSECT-EATING PLANTS FACT FILE

● Round-leaved sundew
Drosera rotundifolia
Habitat and distribution
Common on damp, acidic bogs, especially on bare ground around pool margins throughout much of British Isles
Size 10cm (4in) tall
Key features
Perennial with basal rosette; leaves almost circular, 1cm (½in) across, with many hair-like structures exuding a sticky secretion; leaf stalks hairy but not sticky
Flowering time
July–August

● Great sundew
Drosera anglica
Habitat and distribution
Wetter places than other sundews, in bogs and gravel shores of lakes in East Anglia, Dorset and New Forest, north and west Britain and western half of Ireland
Size Up to 18cm (7in) tall
Key features
Leaves up to 10cm (4in) long and narrow; hair-like structures on leaves but leaf stalks hairless
Flowering time
June–August

● Oblong-leaved or long-leaved sundew
Drosera intermedia
Habitat and distribution
Less widely distributed than other sundews, preferring drier conditions; occurs mainly in north-west Britain and western Ireland, occasionally in New Forest and Dorset
Size 3–5cm (1¼–2in) tall
Key features
Hairy leaves up to 5cm (2in) long, spoon-shaped on long, hairless, erect leaf stalks
Flowering time
June–August

● Common butterwort
Pinguicula vulgaris
Habitat and distribution
Occurs in bogs, on wet heaths, fens and damp mountain slopes in north and west Britain and Ireland; occasionally on higher ground in the south-west
Size 5–18cm (2–7in) tall
Key features
Basal rosette; leaves 2–8cm (¾–3in) long, pointed and oval, pale yellow-green, covered in sticky glands; violet flowers
Flowering time
May–July

● Large-flowered butterwort
Pinguicula grandiflora
Habitat and distribution
Bogs and damp moorland on acidic soils; native to parts of west and south-west Ireland; naturalised in Cornwall, rarely elsewhere
Size 8–20cm (3–8in) tall when in flower
Key features
Similar to common butterwort, but flowers much larger
Flowering time
May–June

● Pale butterwort
Pinguicula lusitanica
Habitat and distribution
In *Sphagnum* bogs and on wet heaths on acidic soils from Hampshire to Cornwall, north and west Scotland and parts of Ireland
Size 3–15cm (1¼–6in) tall
Key features
Smaller than other butterworts; basal rosette; leaves 1–3cm (½–1¼in) long, olive green with purple veins; pale lilac flowers
Flowering time
June–October

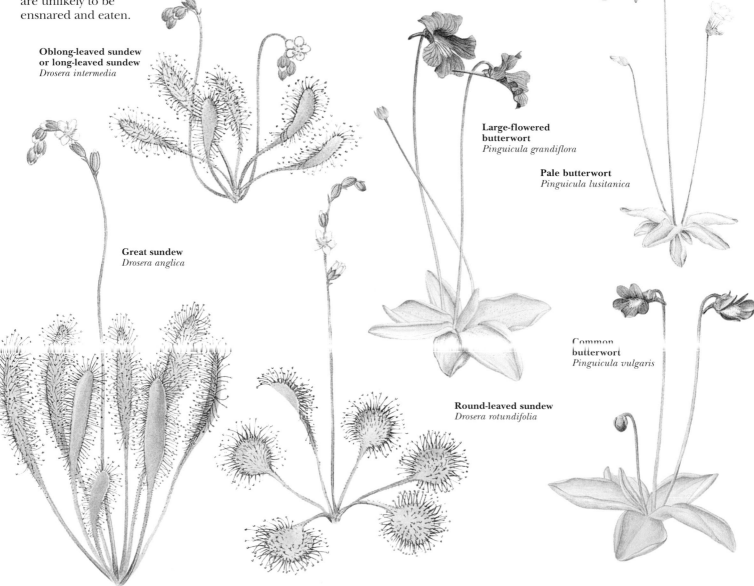

Oblong-leaved sundew or long-leaved sundew
Drosera intermedia

Great sundew
Drosera anglica

Large-flowered butterwort
Pinguicula grandiflora

Pale butterwort
Pinguicula lusitanica

Common butterwort
Pinguicula vulgaris

Round-leaved sundew
Drosera rotundifolia

INSECT-EATING PLANTS FACT FILE

● **Greater bladderwort**
Utricularia vulgaris
Habitat and distribution
Ponds, bog pools and fens, preferring lime-rich water; scattered in much of Britain and Ireland
Size Floating stems up to 45cm (18in) long
Key features
Divided oval leaves 2–2.5cm (¾–1in), green; thread-like leaf segments bear 3mm (⅛in) oval bladders
Flowering time
June–September

● **Wavy bladderwort**
Utricularia australis
Habitat and distribution
Widespread but far less common than greater bladderwort and prefers acidic water
Size Floating stems up to 45cm (18in)
Key features
Mature stems wavy but best distinguished from common bladderwort when in flower; flowers paler and upper lip twice the length of the lower lip
Flowering time
July–August

● **Lesser bladderwort**
Utricularia minor
Habitat and distribution
Scattered across British Isles in peaty bog pools and fen ditches; mainly in north and west
Size Floating stems 8–20cm (3–8in) long
Key features
A slender plant; bristleless leaves 3–6mm (⅛–¼in) long, divided palmately into untoothed segments bearing 2mm (1/12in) long bladders
Flowering time
June–September

● **Intermediate bladderwort**
Utricularia intermedia
Habitat and distribution
Peaty pools in bogs and fens; Dorset, Lake District, Scotland, and western and northern Ireland
Size Floating stems 10–25cm (4–10in) long
Key features
Two types of shoots: floating palmately divided leaves, 3–6mm (⅛–¼in) long, and descending leafless shoots that penetrate the peaty substratum, bearing 3mm (⅛in) bladders (or cups)
Flowering time
July–August

● **Pitcher plant or huntsman's horn**
Sarracenea purpurea
Habitat and distribution
Native to North America; a garden escape or deliberate introduction (as in Roscommon, Ireland, in 1906); occasionally seen on boggy heathland in England and more commonly in bogs of central Ireland
Size 15–60cm (½–2ft) tall
Key features
Evergreen, erect, semi-prostrate rosette-forming perennial; pitchers (leaf tubes) green and purplish red, 20cm (8in) tall; red-purple flowers held well above pitchers
Flowering time
June–July

The yellow-flowered pitcher plant, *Sarracenea flava*, is also grown in gardens. Insects slip on the hairs on the inside of the tube, or pitcher, and fall into the water below.

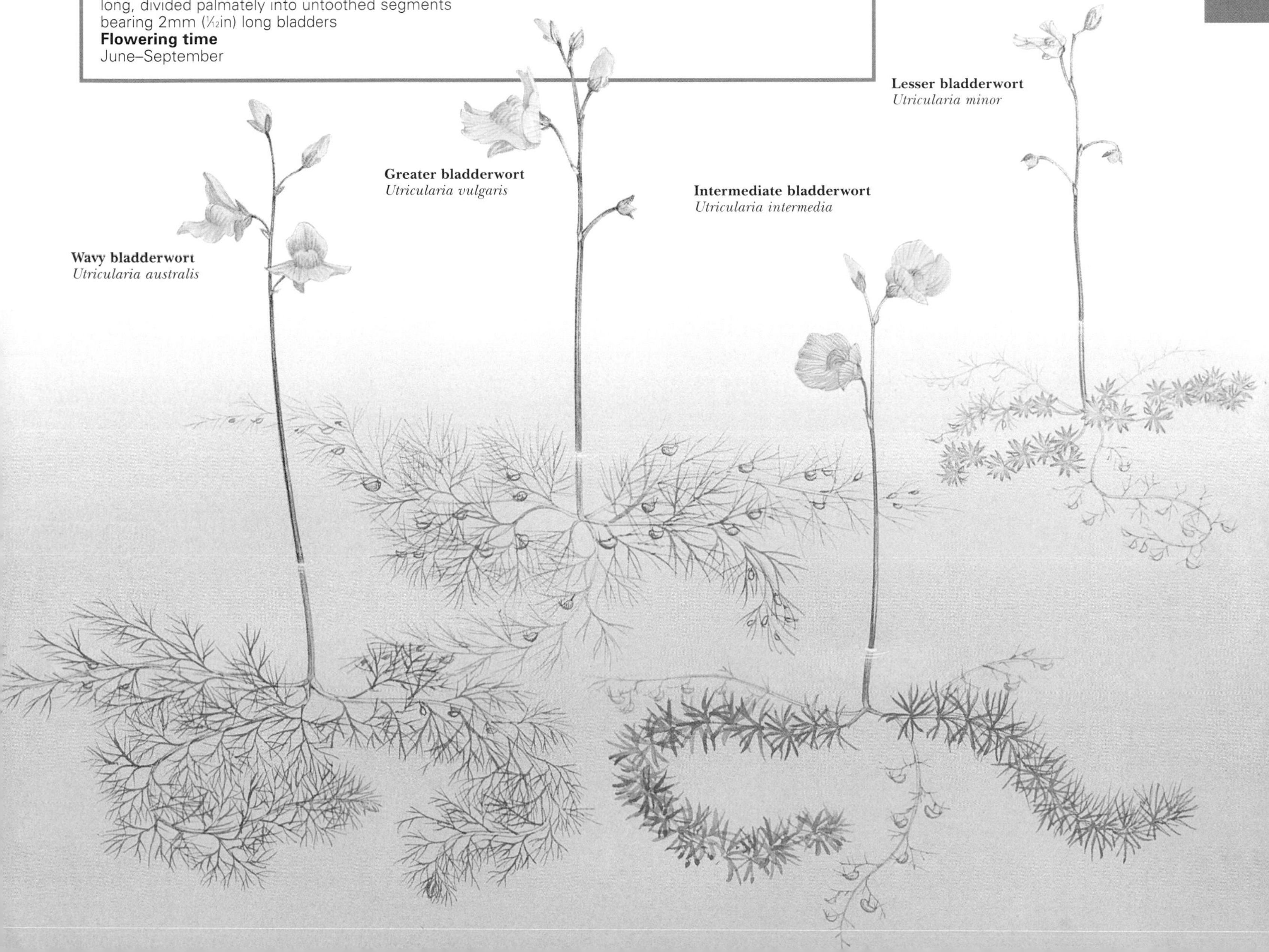

Wavy bladderwort
Utricularia australis

Greater bladderwort
Utricularia vulgaris

Intermediate bladderwort
Utricularia intermedia

Lesser bladderwort
Utricularia minor

Index

Acknowledgments

Photographs: Front cover NHPA/Guy Edwardes, inset RSPCA/N.Rolestone; Back cover Neil McIntyre; 2-3 Woodfall Wild Images/M.Hamblin; 4 FLPA/Michael Callan; 5 (t) NP/A.Cleave, (b) NHPA/D.Heuclin; 6(bl) Windrush/ R.Brooks, (bc) NP/N.Callow, NP; 7(bl) NP, (bc) NP, (br) NP/Paul Sterry; 8(bl) NP, (bc,br) NP/ P.Newman; 9(bl) NP/N.Brown, (bc,br) NP; 10-11 Nature Picture Library/David Kjaer; 12(cl) WW/David Woodfall, (tr) NP/P.Newman, (b) WW/David Woodfall; 13(tl) NP/L.Jessup, (tc) NP/Paul Sterry, (tr) NP/P.Newman, (bc) FLPA/R.Tidman, (b) Laurie Campbell; 14(tr) Laurie Campbell, (cl) FLPA/M.Withers, (cr) Laurie Campbell, (bl) W.S.Paton, (br) FLPA/H.Clark; 15(tr) FLPA/J.Hawkins, (b) NPL/ David Noton; 16(tl) NV/Heather Angel, (tr) NHPA/Laurie Campbell, (b) FLPA/ M.Callian; 17(tc) NP/P.Sterry, (b) NP/P.Sterry; 18(tr) NP/WS Paton, (bl,br) NV/ Heather Angel, 18-19 NV/Heather Angel; 19(inset) NP/A.Cleare; 19(tl) NP/P.Sterry, (tr) NP/P.Newman; (bl) WW/David Woodfall, (br) BC/A.Purcell; 21-22(b) WW/ David Woodfall, 21(c) NV/Heather Angel, (cr) BC/F.Labhart; 22(all pics) NP; 23 NP/A.Cleave; 24 (bl) FLPA/H.Hautala, 24 25 Trip/A.Wright; 25(tl) NP/A.Cleave, (tc) FLPA/M.Nimmo, (cr) WW/A.Gordon, (br) WW/S.Austin; 26(tc) FLPA/I.Rose, (tr) NP/J.Watson, (cr) NV, (bl) FLPA/M.Callan; 27(tr,b) BC/Hans Reinhard; 28(b) BC/J.Cowan, (bl) BC/William Paton, (br) BC/Gordon Langsbury; 29(tr) NHPA/Hellio & van Ingen, (b) NV/Jeremy Thomas, (bcu) BC/Geoff Dore, (bc) BC/George McCarthy, (br) NV/Jeremy Thomas; 30(tr) FLPA/H.Clark, (b) FLPA/ M.Walker; 31(cr) Ardea/S.Undata, (bl,br) FLPA/R.Wilmhurst; 32(tl) Windrush, (tc) Ardea, (tr) Windrush, (bc,br) Ardea; 33(tr) Windrush/D.Green, (c) Ardea/ J.Marchington, (b) FLPA/E&D Hosking; 34(tr,cr,bl,bc) Ardea, (br) FLPA/A.Wharton; 35(tl) FLPA, (b) FLPA/David Sussex; 36(main) WW/M.Hamblin, (cl) NV/Heather Angel, (cr) BC/Gordon Langsbury; 37(tl) NP/H.Clark, (tc) FLPA/ D.Middleton, (tr) BC/Gordon Langsbury, (bc) BC/Hans Reinhard, (br) BC.J.Jurka; 38-39 (main) WW/M.Hamblin, (tl) NP/Frank Blackburn, (c) FLPA/R.Wilmhurst; 39(tl) NV/Heather Angel, (tr) BC/A.Purcell, (bc) NP/A.Cleave, (br) BC/Gordon Langsbury; 40(cl) BC/D.Klees, (tc) FLPA/A.Wharton, (cr) FLPA/I.Rose, (bc) BC/ W.S Paton, 40-41 WW/M.Hamblin, 41(br) FLPA/W.Broadhurst; 42-43 FLPA Images/ Hugo Willcox/Fotura Natura; 44 RSPCA/N. Rolstone; 45(tr) RSPCA/Colin Seddon, (b) NPL/M.Wilkes; 46(tl) Houghton's Horses, (tr) RSPCA/K&P Wolf, (bl) NPL/ Colin Seddon; 47 Ardea/JP Ferrero; 48(tl) RSPCA/N.Rolstone, (tr) FLPA/Silvestris, (b) FLPA/C.Newton; 49(t) FLPA/T.Hamblin, (b) FLPA/D.Middleton; 50 FLPA/ R.Mair; 51 FLPA/R.Mair; 52(tr,cl) NHPA/M.Danneger; 53(tc) NPL/N.Benvie, (cl) FLPA/G.Quedens, NHPA/Laurie Campbell; 54(cl) NHPA/M.Danzigger, (b) NHPA/W.Paton; 55(tr) Aquila, (cl) NHPA/M.Danzigger; 56 BC; 57(r) BC/ Hans Reinhard, (bl) FLPA/R.Wilmhurst; 58(tl) FLPA, (tc) FLPA, (tr) NP, (cl) BC, (c) FLPA, (cr) NP, (bc) FLPA, (br) Mike Read; 59(c) Corbis; 60 FLPA/Michael Callan; 61(t) NPL, (b) NPL/Rico&Ruiz; 62(tc) RSPB, (tr) FLPA/A.R.Hamblin, (cl) FLPA/F.Polking, (c) FLPA/R.Tidman, (bl) FLPA/M.Jones, (bc) FLPA/David Hosking; 64 NHPA/S.Dalton; 65(r) Aquila/J.Simon, (bl) FLPA/R.Wilmhurst; 66(cl) BC/D.Green, (c) FLPA/R.Wilmhurst, (bl) OSF/C.Knights, (bc) FLPA/ R.Chittenden, (br) NP/H.Clark; 67(bl) FLPA/Silvestris, (br) NHPA/S.Dalton; 68(tl,tr) Mike Read, (b) NHPA/A.Williams; 69(tl) Ardea/G.Robbrect, (cr) OSF/ P.Fioratti; 70 Planet Earth/P.Stevens; 71 NP/O.Newman; 72(tl) NP/C.Carver, (cr) NV/Heather Angel; 73(tl) OSF/R.Redfern, (tr) NP/C.Carver, (br) NP/ O.Newman; 74(t) Planet Earth/A.McGeeny, (b) FLPA/F de Nooyer; 75(cl) FLPA/ E&D Hosking, (b) OSF/DG Fox; 76 Gordon Riley; 77(cl) Gordon Riley, (bl) NHPA/ AP Barnes; 78 NS/Richard Revels, (cl,b) NP; 79 NP/F.Blackburn; 80(bl) NP/Paul Sterry; 81(c) NI/Bob Gibbons; 82 Premaphotos; 84(br) Premaphotos; 85 Natural Visions/Heather Angel; 86(l) Still Pictures/John Cancalosi, (br) FLPA; 87 NV/ Heather Angel; 88(t) Mike Read, (c) Pat Morris, (b) Mike Read; 89 NV; 90 (tl) FLPA, (tr) Ardea; 91(tl,tr) FLPA; 92 Neil McIntyre; 93(tr) Neil McIntyre, (c) BC/Dr P Evans, (br) OSF/N.Benvie; 94(tl,bl) OSF/N.Benvie, (tr) Aquila/A.Cardwell, (br) Trip/V.Greaves; 95 Laurie Campbell; 96 Ardea/Z.Tunka; 97 Mike Read; 98(tc) Mike Read, (b) Ardea/Z.Tunka; 99 Ardea/Z.Tunka; 100(cl, c,br) Mike Read, (cr,bl,bc) NHPA; 101(cr) Ardea/Z.Tunka, (b) NHPA/H&V Ingen; 102 FLPA/D.Nill; 103 BC/Hans Reinhard; 104(tl) NPL/S.King, (tr) NPL/D.Welling, (cr) FLPA/M.Jones, (b) NPL/D.Nill; 106(tl) FLPA/J.Watkins, (tc) FLPA/M.Jones, (tr) Mike Read, (cl) NPL/D.Nill, (c) NHPA/A.Williams, (cr) FLPA/D.Hosking, (b) NHPA/A.Rouse; 107(tl) NHPA/D.Watts, (tr) FLPA/J.Watkins, (b) NHPA/A.Rouse; 108 FLPA/ R.Wilmhurst; 109(tr) FLPA/M.Jones, (b) Aquila/W.Lankinen; 110(tl) NP/C.Knight, (tc) Neil McIntyre, (tr) FLPA/T.Hamblin, (cl) Windrush/D.Tipling, (c) NP/ A.Weston, (cr) FLPA/D.Maslowski, (b) NHPA/H&V Ingen; 111 NHPA/R.Tidman; 112(tl) Neil McIntyre, (bl) FLPA/G.Andrewartha, (bc) Mike Read, (br) Aquila/ V.Antonsson; 113(tr) Aquila/G.Bales, (b) Mike Read; 114 NHPA/D.Heuclin, 115(tc) NP/M.Callow, (b) FLPA/G.Moticra; 116(t) Laurie Campbell, (c) FLPA/ R.Chittenden; 117(tl) WW/S.Austin, (tr) NHPA/L.Campbell, (b) NHPA/S.Dalton; 118 NHPA/Laurie Campbell; 119(tr) BC, (cl) OSF/M.Bikhead, (bl) NP; 120(tl) NP, (cl) NSc/R.Revels, (bl) NPL/D.McEwan; 121(tr) NV, (b) Ardea; 122 NV; 124(tr) OSF/P.Parks, (bl) FLPA/Ian West; 125(tr) BC.

Illustrations: 46-47, 52-55, John Ridyard; 59 Midsummer Books; 64 Wildlife Art Agency/Dan Cole; 66-67, 71-74 John Ridyard; 77-78 Midsummer Books; 80-81 Ian Garrard; 83-84 Wildlife Art Agency/Bridgette James; 89-91, 98-100, 105, 111, 112 John Ridyard; 119-120 Midsummer Books; 122, 124, 125 Ian Garrard.

Key to Photo Library Abbreviations: BC = Bruce Coleman Ltd, FLPA = Frank Lane Photo Agency, GPL = Garden Picture Library; NHPA = Natural History Photo Agency, NI= Natural Image, NP = Natural Photographers, NPL = Nature Picture Library, NS = Natural Science Photos, NV = Heather Angel/Natural Visions, OSF = Oxford Scientific Films, PW = Premaphotos Wildlife, WW = Woodfall Wild.

Key to position abbreviations: b = bottom, bl = bottom left, blu = bottom left upper, br = bottom right, bru = bottom right upper, c = centre, cl = centre left, clu = centre left upper, cr = centre right, cru = centre right upper, l = left, r = right, sp = spread, t = top, tl = top left, tlu = top left upper, tr = top right, tru = top right upper.

Wildlife Watch
Moorlands & Uplands in Summer

Published by the Reader's Digest Association Limited, 2005

The Reader's Digest Association Limited
11 Westferry Circus, Canary Wharf
London E14 4HE

We are committed to both the quality of our products and the service we provide to our customers, so please feel free to contact us on 08705 113366, or via our website at: www.readersdigest.co.uk

If you have any comments about the content of our books you can contact us at: gbeditorial@readersdigest.co.uk

® Reader's Digest, The Digest and the Pegasus logo are registered trademarks of The Reader's Digest Association, Inc., of Pleasantville, New York, USA

Reader's Digest General Books:
Editorial Director Cortina Butler
Art Director Nick Clark
Series Editor Christine Noble
Prepress Accounts Manager Penelope Grose

This book was designed, edited and produced by Eaglemoss Publications Ltd, based on material first published as the partwork *Wildlife of Britain*

For Eaglemoss:
Editor Marion Paull
Art Editor Phil Gibbs
Consultant Jonathan Elphick
Publishing Manager Nina Hathway

Copyright © Eaglemoss Publications Ltd/Midsummer Books Ltd 2005

Printed and bound in Europe by Arvato Iberia

CONCEPT CODE: UK 0133/G/S
BOOK CODE: 630-004-1
ISBN: 0 276 44052 8
ORACLE CODE: 356200004H.00.24